Goldmine 1994 Annual

The Standard Reference For Music Collectors

Edited by Bonni J. Miller

Managing Editor: Julie Stuempfig

1993
First Edition
Krause Publications

cover photo by Ross Hubbard—jukebox courtesy Jerry Kopecky, jukebox collector and restorer based in Iola, Wisconsin

Table of Contents

Advertiser Index

Goldmine 1994 Annual

Publisher: Greg Loescher
Editor: Bonni J. Miller
Managing Editor: Julie Stuempfig
Advertising Manager: Jim Felhoffer
Advertising Sales: Sharon Thern
Jeff Warren

ISBN: 0-87341-183-8. Published in the United States of America by Krause Publications, P.O. Box 700, East State Street, Iola, WI 54990, 715-445-2214, publishers of *Goldmine* magazine, the record and compact disc collector's marketplace.

Greg Loescher

Foreword

A Message From Our Publisher

Collectors of recorded music have fallen into three distinct camps the last few years. First are the pure "vinyl junkies" who absolutely have to own the original recording on vinyl. This is basically the backbone of the music collecting hobby. As long as prices for rare vinyl continue to climb, as is amply shown in our three *Goldmine* price guides on albums, 45s and jazz records (see our *Goldmine* book ad elsewhere in this issue), this group will always be around.

The second camp is the collector who still enjoys vinyl records but will buy compact discs to replace their old vinyl copies or when the cost of a particularly rare vinyl recording is prohibitive.

The third camp, mainly younger collectors, are the CD-only collectors who have in many cases never owned a turntable and are not interested in vinyl recordings (yet!).

Of course, this is a simplified grouping – there are other areas to collect – reel-to-reels, cassettes and eight-tracks, for instance – although these represent small slivers of the total collectible market.

Regardless of what type of a collector you are this new *Goldmine 1994 Annual* will definitely hold your interest.

From collecting picture discs, reel-to-reels, to collecting doo-wop, jukeboxes, press kits and promos, these articles on the "subcultures" of mainstream record collecting will give you insight on alternative items you can add to your collection. Our second look at collectible CDs (by *Goldmine* pricing expert Neal Umphred) will also help guide both the novice and advanced collector and dealer in this fast-growing corner of the collector market. With these collector-oriented articles you'll have plenty of reference material to go over during the coming months.

Our main feature article for this year's *Annual* is *Goldmine* editor Jeff Tamarkin's look at the process of reissuing recordings. We constantly receive letters from readers asking why this or that group or artist does not reissue an old recording. Jeff's article gives you the ins and outs (as well as the whys and why-nots) of reissues in an extensive interview with Andy McKaie, MCA Records reissue master.

Speaking of reissues, one of the leading reissue labels, Rhino Records, is also highlighted in this edition of the *Annual* in recognition of their 20 years in the business. My collection contains quite a few Rhino recordings, and yours should also. We're sure you'll find this look at Rhino both entertaining and informative.

We hope the rest of the articles in this edition of the *Goldmine 1994 Annual* provide you with new information and a long-time reference about collecting and music. To update your collection, please patronize our advertisers in this edition. Most also advertise regularly in *Goldmine*, another good reason to start your subscription today!

We appreciate the feedback from readers of our 1st and 2nd editions. So please drop us a line by April 30, 1994, to help us prepare the 1995 edition. Send your comments to: Bonni Miller, *Goldmine*, 700 E. State St., Iola, WI 54990.

Now slap on your favorite recording, sit down in your easy chair, and enjoy your new *Goldmine 1994 Annual.*

Greg Loescher

How – And Why – A Reissue is Made
A Conversation with Andy McKaie of MCA

by Jeff Tamarkin

Andy McKaie hates stamp collectors. Not those perfectly nice folks who take postage stamps and place them in an album, but their record-collecting counterparts. A musical "stamp collector," says McKaie, who oversees all reissues and anthologies released by MCA Records, is a person who doesn't collect for the music but rather for the sake of completing a collection. The stamp collector doesn't care if a record is good or bad, only that he or she owns it in some manner or form. The listening experience isn't nearly as important to this person as the act of collecting itself. The stamp collector may not even listen to the music at all.

In his position as Vice President, Catalog Development & Special Markets A&R for MCA, McKaie has, for the past seven years, heard from a lot of stamp collectors. His instinct is to ignore their obsessions, and concentrate on putting out great music instead.

That he has done. McKaie is one of the rare '90s record company executives whose background is not law school or an accounting firm but a good pair of ears. Long before he began his career in the music industry as a journalist 21 years ago, McKaie was a fan of music, all varieties of music. And now he has a job thousands of collectors must envy: taking that knowledge and love of music and his impeccable taste to work with him every day and making it profitable for MCA by creating high-quality reissues, compilations and boxed sets. He has won two Grammys for doing so (in 1989 for *Chuck Berry – The Chess Box* and in 1991 for *Billie Holiday: The Complete Decca Recordings*).

MCA has made McKaie's job easier for him by giving him access to the catalogs of some of the most important and interesting record labels of past eras. McKaie sifts through the vaults of such historically rich MCA-owned labels as Decca, ABC, Chess, Brunswick, Duke-Peacock and several others for his raw materials and then gets to work presenting that material to a modern, CD-crazed world.

It's not a simple process. Any collector would savor the idea of going into the library of a major record company, picking out favorite albums or songs and putting them onto CDs, but there's more to it than that. There are often legal complications. Sometimes there are physical barriers, such as missing, mislabeled or deteriorated master tapes. It's a dream job, yes, but not one without its challenges.

There is also a balance of interests to be weighed: McKaie – and his counterparts at other companies – is, like anyone else, in business to make money, and must decide not only what music deserves to be in circulation but how to make sure it sells once it's out there. Does an artist deserve a boxed set, a two-CD anthology, a midline release or nothing at all? Is an artist's individual album catalog strong enough to merit reissuing those albums as they were released originally (and are there any left-over songs on those long-hiding tapes that deserve to be tagged on as bonus tracks), or has today's market passed that artist by?

These are decisions that McKaie and the men and women in the "catalog development" departments at every other major label, and many independent labels, must chew over on a daily basis. Those decisions are getting tougher all the time, too, because never has the market for vintage recordings of every conceivable stripe been as strong – or as crowded – as it is now. In the past decade, due largely to the advent of the CD (in addition to other, more intangible factors, such as the alienation of the baby-boom generation from much modern music), an unprecedented boom in reissues has taken place.

Never has so much music, so many different varieties of music, from so many different times and places, been so easily accessible to the consumer. And never has it sounded as good. Collectors can look at the modern reissue as a basic building block of a permanent music collection. In the past, due to shabby releases and the fragile nature of vinyl itself, that was impossible.

In fact, it could be argued that the very definition of the record collector has changed. It used to be easy: A hardcore record collector was someone who sought out original issues,

whether on 78, 45 or LP. Others just sought out the music, in any configuration, thus giving rise to the development of reissue programs, or catalog development, at most labels. Those departments have come a long way.

While the concept of a reissue is nearly as old as the record itself, it wasn't until the late '60s and the '70s that repackagings of older music began to find a real niche in the marketplace. By the early '80s, companies such as Rhino Records, specializing in attractive, intelligently-compiled reissues, took off *[see related article in this volume]*, and other companies devoted strictly to reissues sprang up and found their audience, both in the U.S. and overseas (particularly in Great Britain, Germany and Japan).

The growth of the CD in the mid- to late '80s was matched by the proliferation of reissues, as older record buyers began converting their collections, buying the same albums on compact disc that they'd owned on vinyl since their youth. In doing so, many collectors saw the CD as a more permanent storage medium, and began demanding releases that would be definitive in their content and pristine in their sound. If, as the CD manufacturers argued, the CD would last a lifetime, then CD buyers wanted releases that would never have to be replaced in their lifetime. That meant that an anthology on a given artist would have to contain all of that artist's most important music, and that it would have to sound better than it ever did before—and maybe offer a little something extra.

For the record labels, the CD boom was a learn-as-you-earn (and often a burn-at-every-turn) experience. Most companies now acknowledge that many of their early CD releases, especially catalog reissues, were disastrous, that they both sounded awful and did not make full use of the CD's potential. Indeed, for many labels, the early days of CD reissues consisted of little more than taking already-available titles and switching them over to the new format, without any consideration of sound or other aesthetics. It took the labels some time to realize that the CD medium itself had to be treated differently than the vinyl record, and a little longer still to figure out that they could produce high-quality, highly-profitable reissues extremely inexpensively, as the music that filled them had already been recorded and was sitting in a dusty room somewhere, just waiting to make another appearance.

When consumers started complaining about 30 minutes of music on a 75-minute disc, and lousy sound to boot, the labels finally began smelling impending trouble and retooled their catalog development departments, staffing them with knowledgeable, experienced producers with backgrounds in music and collecting, not necessarily marketing and sales. There was no reason this reissue thing couldn't be done right—the music already existed, and was in demand by buyers. All the labels had to do was determine how best to make it attractive to a more demanding clientele.

By the dawn of the '90s, many of those earlier, poor quality CDs were being pulled from stores and being replaced by superior-sounding, longer, more intelligently programmed collections. Packaging itself improved as well, with scholarly annotation, rare photographs and detailed recording information now standard as opposed to a luxury. Those fly-by-night companies that still attempt to skimp by throwing anonymous-looking, dead-sounding, too-short or just plain lousy, generic reissues up against the elaborate projects spewing forth from the majors and indie specialists, are generally ignored by serious collectors today. Even K-Tel, once considered a joke among serious collectors for its hastily-assembled, novelty-oriented repackagings, is now moving into the business of compiling serious reissues.

Pictured after the *Blues Summit* recording sessions are (l to r): B.B. King; Denny Diante, Vice President, A&R, MCA Records, and Producer of *Blues Summit*; Robert Cray; Andy McKaie, Vice President, Catalog Development and Special Markets, A&R, MCA Records, and Co-Producer/Album Coordinator of *Blues Summit*; John Lee Hooker; Dennis Walker, Producer of "Playin' With My Friends"; and Mike Kappus, Hooker's and Cray's manager.

As we head into 1994, it is apparent that we are in the golden age of the CD reissue, that many of the collections currently on the market will indeed stand the test of time and be considered definitive for decades to come. They are the product of a new generation of collector/compilers employed for the specific purpose of making older music appealing all over again, whether to the fan who lived through it when it was new or the young collector who is hearing it for the first time. All parties seem to agree on one thing: It's got to be done with care; the days of getting away with slapdash reissues is over. Oh, they're still out there all right, but the serious collector can spot them a mile away.

There is, of course, still plenty of differing opinion on how to do it right. How is it decided whether certain music should be reissued at all, whether music that has remained unreleased until now should be taken out of mothballs and finally given an airing? And once the decision is made to assemble a given reissue, how does that project make it from the concept stage to the racks? Is it simply a matter of digging out some old tapes and taking them down to the CD pressing plant? Or is there a magic formula to assembling a successful reissue?

Andy McKaie has witnessed the dramatic growth of the catalog reissue from the inside, and is one of the individuals most responsible for the way we rediscover our old favorites today. As someone who works with a great variety of music from an equally great variety of sources—and as someone who sees the business of selling catalog music from all angles—he is more than qualified to comment on the hows and whys of the reissue business.

Goldmine Annual: In the past decade, since the advent of the compact disc, the surge in catalog reissues has been truly overwhelming. Yet it seems that the vaults are bottomless, because all of the major labels and dozens of indie labels keep coming up with material to reissue.

Andy McKaie: Yeah, that's true. I read the newest issue of *ICE* (a monthly CD newsletter) yesterday and it's unbelievable how many boxed sets are coming out for this Christmas season. It's surreal. It's a dumping ground now.

Goldmine Annual: How long can this continue before there's nothing left to reissue but garbage?

Andy McKaie: I think part of the problem we're having now is not how long it *could* last—it should last a long time because there's a lot of great music out there—but how deep are the pockets?

Goldmine Annual: When the boxed set phenomenon began to gather steam in the mid-'80s, the format was reserved for special material from special artists. Now it seems that every artist that ever sold a few records is getting the box treatment. Doesn't the preponderance of boxed sets dilute their impact?

Andy McKaie: From my perspective, every artist of substance deserves one. For every artist that the critics and the cognoscenti go ga-ga over, there's another one that the general public wants. Do we need another box? Do we need a Steely Dan box? I don't know. But I know one thing: There's a demand for it. And in our system, when there's a demand. you fill it.

In my job, I serve three masters. One is the record company, and what the record company wants to do and how it wants to serve itself and its catalog. Two is the music and what the music, to me, says to do. Three is the general public. They determine where I'm going.

Goldmine Annual: How do you find the balance between what those three masters want? How do you weigh the demands of the general public, the corporate needs and what you want to do?

Andy McKaie: It is a balancing act that I try to do. Of course, when MCA wants something, they get it. For example, they told me they want a Nanci Griffith compilation. So I'll get it for them. It's as simple as that. They want a Steely Dan box, I'll work with them. I make my living working for the company. But I try to do what I think is the best, and the company gives me a lot of leeway. They'll say they want a Steely Dan box and it's left to me to determine the form and all that. If they disagree, they'll say so, or ask questions along the way. But they know I'll try to make it the best I can.

Goldmine Annual: Using the Steely Dan box as an example, after MCA tells you it wants such a project, where do you go next? How do you determine whether it will be two CDs or four CDs or their entire catalog in one package? How do you decide whether to include rarities or just make it a greatest hits package?

Andy McKaie: In this particular instance it has a lot to do with the group. The group has an ongoing relationship with us and they have certain rights, so I have to go to the group and work with them. In other instances, say, the Chess [label] reissues, certain things are left up to me. I have a lot of discretion. I sit around and think about what I'd like to see, if I were on the other side of the coin. What fills what I perceive as the need? I try to not overdo or underdo. I don't generally go for overkill.

But at the same time, I also realize that someone wants something different.

For instance, Buddy Guy is having more success than he's had in a long time and we had two Buddy Guy CDs out. I realized we should do something special for Buddy Guy for Chess. I looked at what was there and realized that what was there would fit on two CDs entirely. It would be something different. There were a lot of tracks that were rare, collectors would love it, and nouveau fans might like it. If they don't, and they want to buy something shorter, they have the choice of going to the individual albums. So I took it from that perspective, and I can still down the line do an edited version of that, geared specifically to the blues people—there's a lot of non-blues R&B in that package. I can make a blues compilation; I knew that at the time I was doing it.

Goldmine Annual: In a sense, you're put in the position of having to continually top yourself, in order to be able to draw customers back to the same music by the same artists. For example, your Steppenwolf compilation, *Born To Be Wild/A Retrospective*, had to be bigger and better than the *16 Greatest Hits* collection that had been out for years.

Andy McKaie: There has to be a reason for its existence. The reason for its existence is that it'll sell. Then you have to give something to people to buy. There are lots of ways of doing that. You can do a short thing and charge little for it, or you can go with the higher end. We did a lot of lower end, midline CDs for a while. For a few minutes we were one of the proponents of that. And by doing that, we put ourselves in a position that, yes, now what I do has to be bigger and better. Any act that I handle, generally, I go for more of the gusto. There's already a best of Bobby Bland out there, so I went deeper. There's already the short form of Buddy Holly, so we did 50 tracks on two CDs.

There's a large audience out there that wants the [larger sets]. The best example of that is the Impressions. We did the short form, it sold a lot, got a nice response, so we came back with the *Anthology* and that sold a lot and got a great response.

Plus, you can upgrade. One thing about this digital era is that it's getting better, thank goodness. The systems are better, we're better—the people who do this thing for a living know more about it, know how to work the systems—and the engineers are better. The companies relate to it a little better.

Goldmine Annual: In the beginning of the CD era, it was sort of a dark age. Record labels didn't know how to use the format to their best advantage so they were treating CDs like vinyl albums. It took a few years for them to understand that there were new possibilities for them to take advantage of.

Andy McKaie: They had no idea. But I think it's like that with any form. And when you have a new market, people want to take advantage of that market and they don't necessarily do it correctly.

Goldmine Annual: After the company upgrades, as you did with the Impressions, does the shorter set stay in print or do you assume everyone is going to go for the bigger package?

Andy McKaie: The early one is still out there, yeah. If I'm going to do something that will supersede, I will pull the early one. Like when we redid the Broadway shows *Oklahoma!, The King And I* and *Carousel*, I had the [older versions] pulled from the marketplace because we were doing better versions of the exact same thing. That's a logical thing to do. But if you're going to do a grandiose, expanded version, there's no reason to take anything off the market. There are people that really only want those 12 songs.

Goldmine Annual: I completely understand that. Sometimes I just want to hear an artist's hits and not another two dozen songs I'm not familiar with. Other times I do want to hear what else they've done.

Andy McKaie: There are plenty of acts I only care about one or two songs. I think you have to judge what the act is worth to the public. Ultimately, that is what it's worth to the record company.

Goldmine Annual: If it was up to *Goldmine* readers, every album by every artist ever recorded would be out in its entirety, with bonus tracks. How much input do you take from the public?

Andy McKaie: I take input, especially if it has any merit or any logic to it. I keep a file with anything I'm thinking about doing. In that file I keep letters and my own notes and sometimes stories I get in the mail. I keep things that will give me hints in the future. I talk to collectors. There is a series of collectors who I respect and take input from. I answer my own phone a lot, as surprised callers have found out. So people can get to me fairly directly, although I prefer them writing a letter. I try to answer my mail, although I'm way behind. I do read everything that comes in, and if a letter comes in that I want to answer, I try to do that right away.

Goldmine Annual: Do you find yourself having to explain to some of these letter writers why certain projects can't happen?

Andy McKaie: Oh, sure.

Goldmine Annual: Okay, what are some of the reasons certain projects can't happen? Is missing master tapes a major one?

Andy McKaie: That's one, but more often than not it's a legal reason, or we don't own the rights anymore. Or we determine that there isn't a market for something.

Goldmine Annual: How do you explain to a fan that an album he loves, and is dying to own on CD, may not be of interest to anyone but himself?

Andy McKaie: It's understandable why he may not understand that. And it's understandable because they see people doing things of a lesser nature than what they're looking for. That's a matter of policy. Every company has its guidelines.

Goldmine Annual: Isn't it true that a project that a major label such as MCA might see as a loser could make money for the right indie label?

Andy McKaie: Absolutely. We license to people like One Way and K-Tel and Era and Razor & Tie. I have no problem with that because I know that if I put them out they'll sink into the sunset.

Goldmine Annual: Is that because your overhead is so high and you'd have to sell more copies to break even than they would?

Andy McKaie: Yeah, plus we can't focus on the small things as well as smaller companies. We're not as hit-driven as some of the other companies because this company is driven by its catalog and does focus on its catalog. I've been doing this for seven years now and we've been focusing on the catalog for years. I'm not the first person to do this here, by far.

Goldmine Annual: What are some of the older labels that MCA now controls?

Andy McKaie: Decca, ABC (which also includes Impulse!, Paramount and Dot), a couple of years' worth of early Brunswick, Kapp, Duke-Peacock, Chess (which includes Aristocrat, Argo, Checker and Cadet) and others. It's a humongous catalog. And what I try to do is keep it varied. I know that I've gained a reputation on a personal level for certain types of music. But at the same time I do keep it varied, I do try to do at least one middle-of-the-road release every year—I have a Bing Crosby box out now—and I do the Broadway stuff as well. We did a Rodgers and Hammerstein box this year. I always try to diversify. I try to keep it coming; I keep Chess going and I keep all the different labels going. We are just really getting into Dot Records. Kapp Records ... they didn't really have much of an identity—*Hello Dolly* was their biggest album—but we're trying to put out a variety of music because there's a variety of marketplaces.

One of the things I try to do is to realize that if you put out too much in one vein, you're going to kill off that vein. I've gotten letters from collectors since I started this job, and in the beginning it was, "Gimme, gimme, gimme, we want, we want." Now it's, "God, this is wonderful, this is incredible, but please make sure they stay in the catalog because I can't afford to buy them all right now." The majority of letters are along those lines. It's overwhelming, especially in the blues field, which we were doing before everyone else started doing it. That's great, but at the same time it's overkill. I know a few of the small labels are getting killed by it and backing off. My next Chess release is a little more pop-oriented, to get away from the blues thing.

Goldmine Annual: I would imagine that the hardcore blues collectors write a lot of letters telling you what they'd like to see. But what about someone like Three Dog Night, who you've just done a package on? Are there people writing in demanding Three Dog Night or did you just make a decision that the time was right for them?

Andy McKaie: I was working my way methodically through the pop artists we've inherited and I believe deserve double CDs. We started with the Mamas and the Papas and then we did Steppenwolf, then Curtis Mayfield and the Impressions, then Wishbone Ash. I'm doing them in a way that I think I can get them done. I'm also putting them out at a point in time that I think is effective. With Wishbone Ash, for example, we put out many of their original albums in midline and they sold very well. At that point I said we should do a compilation, and we did, and it's done fine. We've done Brenda Lee. We've done the artists I think deserve doubles. I still have Joe Walsh and James Gang to do.

We can only do so many at once and I think it's wrong to do too many because you can't focus on them. The salesmen can't. You can only advertise so many at once. Steppenwolf we did along with the Lynyrd Skynyrd box and the Steely Dan *Gold* expanded edition. We advertised it, we focused on the three, we gave deals, and it worked—all three did very well. That's what you want.

To be honest with you, to have 2,000 fans, the freaks, buy something, and it doesn't get outside of there because the company or the dealers can't deal with it, gives me minimal to no satisfaction. I get satisfaction out of the finished product, but I get an even bigger kick when it achieves what I think it should achieve, saleswise. I get disappointed when it doesn't, because that's part of my job.

Goldmine Annual: How much guarantee is there though? An artist may have had a string of 15 Top 10 hits three decades ago and they mean nothing to today's audience. Then you have artists who are much more popular today than when they were recording their music.

Andy McKaie: There are a lot of acts from the '30s, '40s and '50s that don't sell as well as you'd think they would. Al Jolson is one. We did a CD with him because it was the right thing to do and who knows, it might've actually sold. Same thing with Sammy Davis, Jr. But at the same time, this is the right thing to do. You don't always win. Then there's something like the Willie Dixon box, where there was no anticipation of sales. No one knew what it would do—major question mark—and it's a success, a rather huge success. We did the Brady Bunch earlier this year, and no one thought it would do much, and it took off.

Goldmine Annual: We've talked mostly about anthologies. How does the process differ when you work with a straight reissue of an old album, a group like the Who, for example?

Andy McKaie: I try to put out the most popular stuff and work my way through it. Sometimes there are legal problems and it takes a long time. The *American Graffiti* soundtrack took us three years because we had to re-license everything on it. Some people who are no longer on the label have a residual, and when you talk to them they're not happy and they give you tsuris. That's understandable. I try to balance what I think will sell. When it comes to what's going to sell in a reissue, the outside influence is really important to me. I do respect it. The MCA salesmen are also really on top of it; they do all the dirty work. They often say, "Put so and so out," and they're sure enough right.

Goldmine Annual: What about the other extreme, something you feel strongly should be released, even though you know it won't sell in great numbers? For example, you did a Chess release on Sugarpie DeSanto, a female R&B singer who is hardly remembered at all today.

Andy McKaie: That one actually did pretty well. There were a couple of lesser Chess names that didn't do too well, but that one did. I felt it should be out there. We were doing a lot of Chess stuff at the time and that was one of many we put out. Chess is looked at as an overview, so if we have a clinker here or there it doesn't really matter. It's the label itself that we've been working; we're rebuilding up the name.

Nobody was that familiar with Sugarpie but she did pretty well. Not enough to go back for another helping, but reasonably well. It's actually outsold some other things with big hits on them. What happened there was the press kicked in. If the press kicks in you can do halfway decent numbers on a relatively unknown thing. You get a review in *Rolling Stone*, a review in *Goldmine* and a review in a couple of other places, there's an interest where there wasn't before. It wasn't like the press got onto it from a point of, "Gee, this is interesting from a historical point of view." They got onto it from a point of, "This is good. You will enjoy it." That got a few more people motivated than would've been otherwise.

Goldmine Annual: You put out a single CD package of Muddy Waters' plantation recordings from the early '40s. That's an example of one that is historical in nature but also got phenomenal press.

Andy McKaie: There's some great music there too, but it's done very much from a historical point of view. It also got airplay on college and public broadcast stations.

Goldmine Annual: That's a whole different approach to reissues: the completist approach, where you include everything from a given period, including alternate takes. Labels such as Bear Family and Mosaic specialize in that approach, but American major labels almost never do.

Andy McKaie: You can do that on a mass market level with certain kinds of artists. Muddy Waters is one. He is an artist who generally sells very well. He's probably the best-selling artist in the Chess catalog. Chuck Berry's *The Great Twenty-Eight* is the biggest-selling item in the Chess catalog but *Best Of Muddy Waters* is number two. And by far, the Muddy Waters box is the biggest-selling box. Muddy Waters is someone you can take that [completist] approach with because he is revered and he is well known and he sells records. You can still sell and you can still serve the music very well. You're doing a great service to history and collectors. There's a lot of history in that package. MCA bent over backwards for that and I'm very proud of what we did. I got MCA to do things that, five years ago, I didn't even dream of having MCA do.

Goldmine Annual: Five years ago I remember a certain label saying they would never do any reissues on a certain band because there was no market for them, and now they've got the whole catalog out.

Andy McKaie: The market is wonderful, because of the CD boom and because of the older generation of people getting into the market. There are extremes in the market now, like rap and metal, and you never had a schism like that before. Think back to psychedelia. What was the counter? Blues, singer-song-

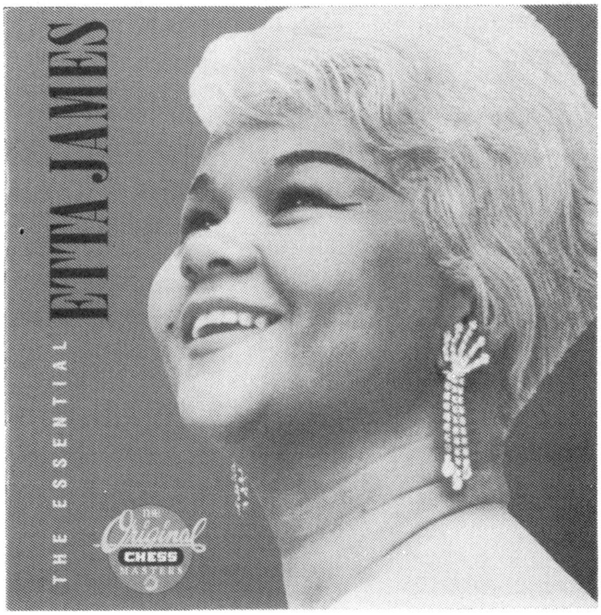

writers. Now we have rap and metal. What's the counter? Blues, singer-songwriters.

Goldmine Annual: I don't know if that comparison holds. When you heard a psychedelic band in the '60s, and they were covering a Muddy Waters song, you wanted to know who Muddy Waters was and to hear his version of it. There was a link. But when you hear a rap tune, do you go and seek out the artists being sampled? Do rap fans care about their artists' influences?

Andy McKaie: Yeah, okay. But right now, we probably have the most fractionalized marketplace for records that there has been since records began. The fractions are selling big numbers, because there are so many people in the marketplace. I do think, though, that we're all putting out some good stuff but we're all shooting ourselves in the foot, too.

Goldmine Annual: Why is that?

Andy McKaie: Because we're putting too much out. There's no way in hell I'd be able to afford all this stuff if I was outside of this.

Goldmine Annual: Up until a few years ago we were able to keep track of most of the reissues coming out, but now we can only review a fraction of them in *Goldmine*, because there are simply too many. And like you said, a lot of them are good, but we still have to pick and choose, so even some of the important packages are not getting covered.

Andy McKaie: I think the value of a positive review is losing its effect, to a degree. Everybody's writing about what they like, because there's so much to choose from, especially in reissues. If you have someone who likes an act, they're generally going to get a favorable review. It's not at the point of saturation but this Christmas it might be, with all the boxes.

Goldmine Annual: I made up a list of every anthology of two or more CDs that came out in 1993, and there were close to 200 of them. How many can the average collector buy, five or 10 at most?

Andy McKaie: That's why I try to get some out early, so we at least get a chance in the marketplace. People can only spend so much in a record store. I'm finishing up my seventh year here, and I've watched it mushroom. Now that Warner Bros. is officially in the fray, it's going to get worse. I know of a couple of labels that've backed off. One of my main competitors was finished with its reissues for the year in mid-year.

Goldmine Annual: Do you think some of the labels are guilty of throwing unnecessary product out on the market just to justify keeping their jobs? Are they paying too much attention to the demands of collectors and not enough to what the market really needs?

Andy McKaie: The problem I have with a lot of collectors is that they've become what I call stamp collectors. They don't care about the music anymore. All they want is to be able to check off in their Whitburn book [Note: Joel Whitburn publishes books based on the *Billboard* charts] or their discographies and be able to say, "I have this." I call these people stamp collectors, mainly because, with stamps, you don't care what the quality of stamps is, you've just got to fill that page.

A stamp is a stamp, but that's not how it is with music. The same artist at the same session can have a clinker or a winner.

I have an example. Florence Ballard [one of the three original Supremes] made an album and when I took this job I started getting inundated with Florence Ballard and Supremes fan club people asking me for this album. The album is unreleased; I think there was one single from it. I went and listened to the record and there's a reason it didn't come out. If ABC didn't release something, there's a real reason. When I listened to it, I found out why – it's a very bad record. It's very unfortunate.

So my decision was that it wouldn't help her memory. The woman has a very good reputation and this would hinder it. I decided not to put it out and I played it for a few people and they agreed and they backed off. However, the stamp collectors will never back off.

I made a decision on the Brenda Lee collection, not to include a song called "Think." I was surprised it was so bad. I asked Brenda and her husband what they thought and they said, "Well, you notice we've never had it put on any albums either." It was a #25 hit but it was dreadful. The engineer, when he heard it in the studio, asked to be excused. So anyway, we put out the double CD, and immediately I start getting inundated with the stamp collectors who wanted their "Think." One of them made the mistake of putting his letter on stationery that had his phone number, so I called him up and he was very taken aback.

I said to him, "Have you ever heard the song?" And he said no – most of these people have never heard these songs. I said, "Well, it's dreadful." And he said, "I don't understand that." I would be doing a disservice to him and the package and everyone else if I put it on.

Someone else might do it differently. There's another reissue producer out there who put out an album with bonus tracks that were dreadful. A great album, but bad bonus tracks. I asked him why he did that and why he ruined the listening experience, and he said, "Because the collectors want it."

Goldmine Annual: How do you feel about reissues that have studio dialogue stuck in the middle of the music? Pete Howard of *ICE* wrote an interesting article on that subject for *CD Review*. Some of the reissue producers love having it in there because they feel it gives the listener a taste of the atmosphere in the studio, and others, like Rhino's Gary Stewart, think it's a travesty, that it interrupts the listening experience.

I happen to agree with Gary. When I put on a CD of music, I want to hear the music. I don't want it interrupted by people jabbering in the studio. I don't find it interesting or germane to the music. Big deal that they were talking. For example, in a recent Sony/Legacy compilation, a classic album has bits of stoned chatter between tracks. That to me is like breaking up *Sgt. Pepper* with the guys asking for a cup of tea or something.

Now the new Paul Simon boxed set on Warners has a couple of minutes of something called "The Breakup," which is not a song but a tongue-in-cheek routine where Art Garfunkel talks about his split with Paul Simon while Simon eggs him on. It may be funny the first time but do I really want to hear it every time I feel like hearing the Paul Simon music on that CD? No. I think if compilers have to put dialogue on, for whatever reason, they should put it at the end of a disc.

Andy McKaie: You have to use judiciousness when it comes to that.

Goldmine Annual: Right. I'm not talking about the producer saying "Take three" before the music begins, I'm talking about conversations that were insignificant then and are insignificant now.

Andy McKaie: I find "Take three" more offensive. At least the other gives you some personality. I find slates, with an engineer calling a number ... give me a break. That's the worst. I find that absolutely offensive. As far as dialogue goes, I try to be judicious. I also try to bracket it if I can, so you can skip over it.

Goldmine Annual: That's a good point, because most of the reissues that contain dialogue don't index it so the listener can program it out – it's just stuck there and you have to sit through it every time. But even if it is indexed, who's going to take the time to program a CD player just to skip over two minutes of talking? For example, if you were going to decide to put some studio dialogue into the Who's *Tommy*, you wouldn't put it between two songs, you'd probably stick it at the end somewhere.

Andy McKaie: With a compilation you have a little more leeway than a straight reissue. But at the same time, you have to think of what it does to the package, what it does to the song. Sometimes it helps, sometimes it hinders. You have to turn yourself into a listener. I went apeshit once. I got somebody's compilation once and, following a gorgeous ballad from the '50s – I'm listening through headphones at home – you hear [in a booming, distorted voice], "Master take 26." I jumped up and if the producer was there I would've killed him. It was two seconds after the music died. There's no rational reason for

that.

That's a stamp collector. A stamp collector doesn't listen to the music. All he cares about is authenticating the experience and checking off that he got this. He doesn't go back and listen to this stuff; it's not in permanent rotation in his house. He doesn't have a permanent rotation is his house. They just accumulate, and it really bugs the daylight out of me.

I do understand some of the collector mentality. Most of the people I deal with on all ends are collectors of some sort. I am too; I came from a collector background. But at the same time, I also am a listener and I love this music. I'm not gonna screw my listening experience. I don't want, at the beginning of the song, some jackass ruining it for me. I care about transitions; that's part of the making of a record.

Goldmine Annual: I wonder if some of these compilers consider the setting in which people actually listen to music. You're sitting in your living room or eating dinner or driving in your car, and the music is playing along nicely. Maybe you are paying close attention or maybe your thoughts are elsewhere or you're having a conversation. And then when you expect one song to fade out and the next to begin, you hear some guy yell "Take 47" and it jars you. All of a sudden it's not music anymore; it's a document of a recording session. Does the listener really care what take it is or what they were eating for lunch that day in 1958?

Andy McKaie: Right, although I actually included, in a Bo Diddley CD, Bo Diddley ordering lunch (laughs). But the thing is, that's the kind of insight you can put on a box or certain kinds of rarities packages, that is effective to a degree, especially if it's not interfering in the overall enjoyment of it. What I find offensive is when they use slates that are *non sequiturs,* talk that has no personality to it, just to have talk on a record. I don't particularly like putting things around classics. I try not to do that. If you have a classic piece of music, let the music talk for itself.

Once in a while, you can pull off something with a flair, but you've got to be careful. I like to bracket the dialogue. On quite a few packages I've put dialogue on, like the Muddy Waters plantation thing, you can skip right over it.

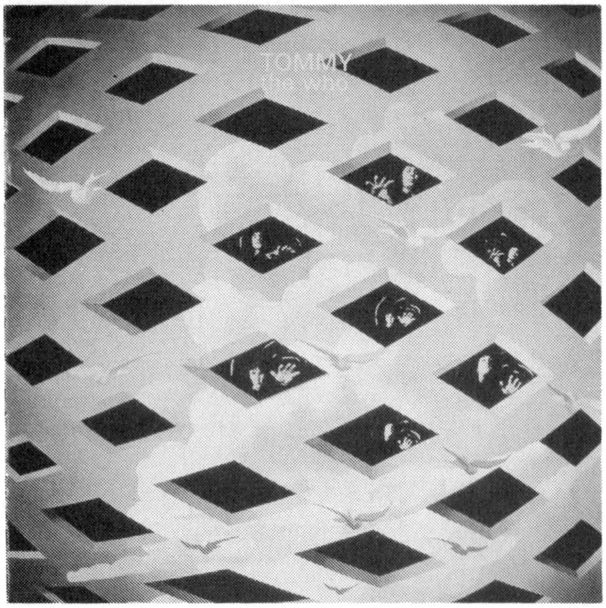

Goldmine Annual: That's a bit of a different situation. With the Waters release [*The Complete Plantation Recordings – The Historic 1941-42 Library Of Congress Field Recordings*], that dialogue is part of what you are buying, it's integral to the recorded work. Those recordings were done in the field, and the interviews are as much a part of the story as the music.

Andy McKaie: Right. In certain types of things, the dialogue is offensive. It interferes with the flow of the music.

Goldmine Annual: We've talked about the whys behind a reissue but not the hows. After you come up with the concept for a release, what are the steps you take next to implement it? For starters, a lot of collectors have a romantic notion of going into a huge vault filled to the brim with dusty old tapes, some of which contain incredible unreleased music no one has ever heard. Are all of MCA's tapes really in a vault?

Andy McKaie: We have an airplane hangar that we share with the film company here [Universal]. It really is a monstrous vault. It's very high so we have a lift truck that goes up and down and it's air conditioned, kept to a certain temperature and humidity. It literally prints out computer printouts on itself every day. It's a high-end system that I'm trying to encourage other record companies to do. A lot of record companies rent vault space in very questionable places. This is relatively new for us. The record company and the film company got together about six years ago and did it. The interesting thing is that even when I find tapes that have been sitting in someone's house for years, when I put it in our vault, a year later I take it out, and the oxides actually adhere better.

Goldmine Annual: Let's take a specific package, the B.B. King boxed set *King Of The Blues*. How did that go from the concept stage to the stores?

Andy McKaie: I decided to take a look at what he'd done and decided it should be four CDs. I realized that the scope of his career was that grand. And I also thought that from a commercial standpoint, going any more than four you would be running into a price point that would probably hurt him. As it was, it still ended up selling from $55-62, which is expensive. But at the same time, that's not as expensive as $75-80.

I had met and spoken to Colin Escott, and his partner David Booth, and they both had great knowledge of Memphis and B.B. King. So I approached them about being involved and they jumped at the chance. They got together and listened to records and came back to me with cassettes of things they thought should be on the package. They came up with a basic outline.

Goldmine Annual: What was their criteria? Do you start by looking at chart figures to make sure that all of the major records are included?

Andy McKaie: They had a mixed criteria. They were trying to balance hits and things they thought were really good and what was reflective of his career. I took what they did and went to the vault and had everything pulled. Then I listened to virtually every tape that I could lay my hands on and put together my own track listing and, finally, Colin, David and I discussed the differences between the two track listings and came up with a compromise package that we were all happy with.

Goldmine Annual: What kind of condition were the tapes in?

Andy McKaie: Of all the ABC artists, his were probably in the best condition. They also suggested, and I had listened to, some of the early recordings for Modern Records and then I ran around and started to license. It was a little more complicated than usual because the early recordings by him are owned by different people in different sections of the world.

Goldmine Annual: Can you explain exactly what licensing is? For example, you wanted material cut for Modern in the early '50s. How do you go about finding out who owns the rights to it and then get the use of it for your project?

Andy McKaie: You find out just by being in the business; you just know. You know who's putting out which reissues, what their rights are, and if you don't know you call them up. Rhino is a good source because they deal with everybody. If I don't know where to go for something I'll call them up and often they'll have an idea.

Goldmine Annual: Is it more difficult for you to license because you work for a major label than it would be for someone like Rhino?

Andy McKaie: Yes. There's the element of deep pockets. People think that because we're MCA we have enough to line deep pockets. There's also the element of competitors who are cautious about what they'll license to you because they'll want to deal with it too. With B.B., the first track was from Bullet Records and it was very interesting to find out who owned Bullet Records at this point. Finally, we found Mrs. Bullet. She was thrilled and we cut a deal with her.

All the Modern stuff is owned by Virgin in America, Ace in England and Blues Interactions in Japan, so we had to deal with that and cut separate deals with each of them. Some of the duets had to be cleared through management companies and

other record labels. U2 and [PolyGram's] Bill Levenson helped me get the single edit of "When Love Comes To Town," which B.B. cut with U2. I knew there were several edits and Bill got me all the different edits.

Goldmine Annual: The legal part is half the battle.

Andy McKaie: The legal part is a pain, because once you give someone the idea that you want something from them, oftentimes they feel, whoops, this is valuable. Then they exaggerate that value. If they're part of the we license to you, you license to us network, then it's easy. But if they're just newcomers and don't understand it, or they're oldcomers and they want to be greedy about it, it can be a pain. Some just don't want to give away what they have. Generally, most of the record companies are licensing from each other these days.

Goldmine Annual: If you'd stuck to material owned solely by MCA for the B.B. box, it would've gone much smoother.

Andy McKaie: And it would've been out much sooner.

Goldmine Annual: What else is involved in the planning, other than securing licenses?

Andy McKaie: We contacted B.B. and his manager, Sid Seidenberg, and we started talking about content and the music in it. Colin Escott and I went over to Vegas to B.B.'s house, and we did an interview with B.B. for the box, and we also spent about another hour or two just playing music for each other and talking about the content and the music, why things would be on it and why not.

Goldmine Annual: Did he have certain music he wanted to include?

Andy McKaie: Oh, yeah. He played us certain things and I played him a few of the oddball things I had found, like "Sloppy Drunk," which he fell apart in hysterics when he heard it. He just fell over. He didn't remember doing it but he thought it was funny. He also went through credits with us, because we had begun to do our research for the credits. He came up with some nice input on that. Then we had dinner and talked and he came in with some good, solid advice.

He was the one who suggested that jazz track, "Don't Get Around Much Anymore." He knew that was a track that we wouldn't know, and he was right.

After that day, I honed the package down, and honed it down some more. You have to figure out minutes-per-side and that sort of thing. It was chronological. I went through books and found an ABC Records sessions book that helped me with some of the research and the chronology.

Goldmine Annual: Are these log books that the labels kept?

Andy McKaie: Yeah, all of them are different. Some are pretty informal, just a three-hole looseleaf with dates and sessions and numbers and sometimes telling you where it is. But I found it and went through it and started making calls. I called Sun Studios to find out when B.B. was in there with U2, and they told me. I called B.B.'s manager, Sid Seidenberg, for some information. I called [producer] Don Was because he hadn't put down the personnel on his track ["Right Time, Wrong Place," with Bonnie Raitt]. I found B.B.'s conductor, Johnny Pate, and asked him a whole bunch of questions. Then we started putting the photos together.

Goldmine Annual: Does MCA have its own photo files?

Andy McKaie: We have some. It's different with every artist. With Lynyrd Skynyrd we have tons. With B.B. we were okay but not so hot. But our art director made some phone calls and I made some and things started showing up. Vartan designed the cover. We brainstorm on covers. Like for the Skynyrd box, Ron O'Brien, who co-produced the box, brought in a picture of a swamp and said, "This would be an interesting starting point for the graphics." Vartan took one look at it and said, "Got an idea."

Goldmine Annual: How do you decide on liner notes writers?

Andy McKaie: Colin Escott was the logical choice for the B.B. box. He was part of the compilation and also he's a very good writer. You come in contact with a lot of writers, you talk to them, you know what their taste is. Often they get involved a little further than liner notes. Little by little, my circle of liner notes writers keeps expanding. The easiest thing to do, when you do what I do, is to have a stable of writers who you can give an assignment and push a button and they go. There are guys like Todd Everett, who likes wacko projects; he likes taking on projects because he finds them interesting: "I've never written about that." On occasion, I like to bring in some of my bigger-name friends who write.

Goldmine Annual: You have a background in journalism yourself, right?

Andy McKaie: I started out in the business in 1972 with tear sheets from an underground newspaper in Norfolk, Virginia, and walked around Manhattan with the addresses of *Rock* magazine, *Crawdaddy* and a couple others. I literally sat in the lobby at *Crawdaddy* and had Peter Knobler, who was the reviews editor at the time, read my clips. He read them and called me in and he said, "You're a good writer, what do you want to do?" That was how I began. Then I was an editor at [Long Island rock tabloid] *Good Times* and a staff writer at London records and then a publicist for Arista. I used to do liner notes myself.

Goldmine Annual: How did you learn how to put together a reissue?

Andy McKaie: From Bob Porter. [Note: Porter is a producer and disc jockey with a vast knowledge of jazz and R&B; he's compiled reissues for such labels as Savoy and Atlantic.] Bob used to come in and talk to me when he was doing the Savoy reissues and I was a publicist at Arista. I'd see what he was doing and read the stuff. He did some absolutely wonderful reissues. I've always liked music—I started buying records when I was eight years old.

Goldmine Annual: Do you have people who work with you on

all of your projects?

Andy McKaie: I don't have a fact-checker or anything like that. I don't even have a staff, just an assistant. But I do my own research. Sometimes I have help: Gary Stewart of Rhino helped me with the Three Dog Night research. I like having a lot of information in my packages.

Goldmine Annual: This is history you're chronicling, and it should be as correct as possible. There's so much misinformation out there and it keeps getting recycled because of lazy researchers and writers.

Andy McKaie: There's two ways to look at it: It's history and it's music. The history end of it has to be served and the musical end of it has to be served. The history end should be served by giving the person as much background as possible, and the music end of it should be served by the sound being as good as it can be, and by picking the best musical tracks. You don't always pick the tracks that you want to hear. The hits have to be there, unless they're offensive.

Goldmine Annual: What would you describe as an offensive hit?

Andy McKaie: I just did a Pat Boone compilation and I left quite a few out. I left out "At My Front Door," "Long Tall Sally" and "Tutti Frutti."

Goldmine Annual: All of his rock 'n' roll covers. Why?

Andy McKaie: I felt that, in 1993, most people know the originals of those songs real well, and they don't want to hear those covers. He had a lot of hits, so it wasn't like we had to scramble.

Goldmine Annual: Most people who'd buy a Pat Boone compilation probably don't want to hear rock 'n' roll anyway.

Andy McKaie: Exactly. The stamp collectors will be offended, but I gave those records to Pair Records and they put them out. I just felt this was the most listenable package for someone who would be interested in Pat Boone now. It's a simple, straightforward greatest hits. I did the same with Judy Garland and the Ink Spots and it worked. Again, I have nothing against those [rock] records by Pat Boone—I'm not making these [compilations] for myself. But I have to be pleased with it, to be able to listen to it and say it's the best product we could do. It's not something I have to be able to take home and play.

My attitude about reissues is that you should be able to look at what I put out and not be able to tell what I like and don't like. I should be serving the music and the public.

But I also think there is a point where you say, this is the right thing for this music at this time. And I think that's what we did with Pat Boone.

Goldmine Annual: Getting back to the assembly of a package, what happens next after you locate your master tapes?

Andy McKaie: You find the songs you want to do and start sorting through the tapes. What I also did with B.B. is I went through multi-tracks and found unreleased material and unmixed material. Or I found roughly mixed material that needed to be remixed. I went in and remixed some of it. I got Bill Inglot involved and he remixed some of it. [Note: Inglot is known as one of the best engineers/remixers in the reissues business; he has worked on hundreds of projects for Rhino and other labels.]

ABC Records was generally not in very good shape. But in B.B.'s case, he had a special position at ABC. Coltrane did too. A few of the artists they viewed as long-term artists and they kept their tapes in pretty good shape.

Goldmine Annual: Do you sometimes have to do major repair work on tapes?

Andy McKaie: In this case there was one thing that Colin Escott and David Booth wanted on, which I wasn't familiar with, which was the complete single version of "Sweet Sixteen." It was a live version that, for whatever reason, when they went to put it on an album, they chopped off the intro. I never found the intro or the multi-track or anything. So I went to Steven Lasker, who does my transfers and my pre-tape research, and asked him if he could find a mint condition of that single, and he did. He not only found that the intro was missing but the outro on the original single was missing.

So we transferred the single, then we digitally reconstructed the entire thing, superimposing the master onto the vinyl transfer. You can do that with our systems today.

Goldmine Annual: How often do you have to resort to methods like that?

Andy McKaie: More than I'd like to.

Goldmine Annual: Are the tapes usually there or are a lot missing?

Andy McKaie: A lot are missing. It could range from 10 or 20 percent to something like the Bing Crosby box, where it's 40 or 50 percent. You have to rely on clean vinyl or acetates. Luckily, Decca, in the '40s, right to the beginning of the analog tape phase, they were still cutting safeties on acetate. That's why the Billie Holiday sounds so good. But the pre-'42 you go to metal, you go to vinyl. You do what you have to do. Every song is different.

Goldmine Annual: So when you get letters from people asking for a certain project, they don't always have a clue just how difficult it would be for you to honor that request.

Andy McKaie: I didn't have a clue either. The mastering end of it, just going through tapes and figuring out the right take, is a pain in the neck. I don't know every take. You try to find the release version and then you do a lot of A-B'ing. But you can even get faked out there because there'll be something that you missed that's different. [Note: The process of A-B'ing involves taking two seemingly identical sources and playing them simultaneously, switching between the two, in order to make comparisons.] There are millions of mixes of things.

KINESIS INC.
1430 Wisp Ct
Hanover, MD
21076 USA
Tel/Fax:
(410) 551-8081

Distributed in USA
by Smashing
Records
Tel: (708) 782-1877
Fax: (708) 782-1893

FREE CATALOG

CASTANARC - Journey to the East
MULTI-STORY - East/West
CRAFT - Craft
FONYA - Wanderers of the Neverending Night
CATHEDRAL - Kingdom of Ends
HAZE - In the End: 1978-1988
FONYA - Soul Travels
Coming soon: ILUVATAR
new CATHEDRAL

KINESIS

International Sinatra Society

P.O. BOX 7176
LAKELAND, FLORIDA 33807-7176
☎ 1-813-646-7650

6 News Magazines per year - ALL SINATRA!
Each issue is 32 pages (8x11 inches) every two months.
Full color front cover, and loaded with photos inside.
Collectors Column features rare collectibles.
Concert reports and reviews.
Official Press releases.
Latest CDs, videos & Laserdiscs.
Sinatra's Concert Schedule & Calendar.
Discounts and special offers.
Auction and Tape Club offerings with each issue.
Personalized Membership card when you join.

$20. US/Canada, all others $25. AIRMAIL delivery!

Twenty page, GIANT Newspaper Size CATALOG full of Sinatra items $3.00
FREE CATALOG to NEW MEMBERS when they join!
Join today or send $5 for CATALOG & SAMPLE ISSUE.

We also BUY your rare Sinatra items and WE PAY TOP PRICES!

MINIATURE 14k GOLD RECORDS & CDs

These incredible handmade works of art have all the detail of their lifesize counterparts. Every groove is there!

The carefully engraved label on the 78 reads Old Time Sound 78 RPM. The 45 reads 14-k Golden Oldie 45 RPM by 4 Star Creations, and the LP reads Big Hits Stereo LP Vol. 1-Side 1.

You'll really enjoy wearing and looking at these unusual and beautiful pieces. They may be worn as pendants, charms or earrings.

Custom label work and engraving on back is available at extra cost. Call or write for quote.

Send $2.00 for my exciting musicians catalog.

Here's How To Order:

Specify pendant, charm or earring size Sm ¾" $50. ea.; Med. 1" $75. ea.; Lg. 1½" $150. ea. Pay by check or money order. 14k gold quality and satisfaction guaranteed. NY res. add 8.5% tax. Add $5.00 shipping & handling.

Send To **4 STAR CREATIONS**
18 Horseshoe Lane, Commack, NY 11725 or call 516-864-7044

ALBUMS-45s-TAPES
COMPACT DISCS-BOOKS-VIDEO
COLLECTABLES-MEMORABILIA

New Orleans Rhythm & Blues

World's Largest & Best Selection

South Louisiana Rhythm & Blues

1947 to present
Swamp R&B, Swamp Pop, Cajun, Zydeco
Terrific Catalogs
$3 USA & Canada
$5 Foreign

Other Ace Catalogs

Soul-Blues-R&B L........ $3
Country-Western-Folk Bluegrass LPs........ $2
Comedy LPs........ $2
Male Pop & Rock vocal Lps........ $2
Female Pop & Rock Vocal LPs........ $2
Rock & Pop Groups LPs........ $3
Movie Sound Tracks Orig Cast........ $2
Jazz, Big Band, Instrumental LPs........ $3

All The Above $5, Foreign $8
Want Lists May Be FAXed to 601-374-4645

ACE VIDEO & MUSIC, INC.

285 Caillavet St., P.O. Box 1934
Biloxi, Mississippi 39533-1934 USA
(601) 374-0777, FAX (601) 374-4645

Goldmine CUSTOMER SERVICE

Goldmine Annual: Let's talk about mixes, because that's a touchy point with collectors. If it's not exactly the same mix that they remember from the radio hit, they can get awfully upset.

Andy McKaie: That's part of the problem in dealing with all the labels, is that they didn't give a damn about keeping what they felt was a single that was already gone. The album was important, not the single. In ABC's case, most of the singles are long gone. They were destroying their own tapes in the '70s because they didn't want to pay for storage. For example, with the Mamas and the Papas there were several single mixes that were vastly superior to the album mixes and I wanted to use them. I couldn't find them; they don't exist as far as I know.

Goldmine Annual: Sometimes you just have to go with what you have, even if it's not the mix you want.

Andy McKaie: Absolutely. On the Etta James CD I put out [*The Essential Etta James*], the mix of "Security" I like using is the only real good stereo mix. I saw one note that said, "An aborted version of attempting to make the stereo sound like a single." It's the same mix, it's just that it's the stereo, which they'd never heard.

I am of a mind that you don't remix if you don't have to. I've done it but it's for a specific reason.

Goldmine Annual: When Motown put out its first *Hitsville* box last year, and all of the tracks were in mono, they took a lot of heat from collectors who said, "But it exists in stereo!"

Andy McKaie: Motown had a tendency to use different takes for mono and stereo. It would be like if I did the Pat Boone with all the stereos on it. They were different takes, recorded at different times. We only used stereo on a couple. The hit versions are the hit versions, and the stereo versions happen to be the stereo versions. It's a value judgment.

Billy Stewart is a prime example. The single mono version of "I Do Love You" is a different take than the stereo version. It's a different approach, a different mood. I've used both. On *One More Time*, the collection of his things, it's in mono, and on *Classic Soul* it's stereo. Both of them are good. The stereo has been on every album, but the mono is probably a little superior, a little bit tenser and more like a single. I didn't know it was different; it was pointed out to me.

I take that into consideration. That's why I hire people who are more knowledgeable than me in an area. The thing is that most collectors who are knowledgeable and also do this want all the loose ends put in, just like the collector outside, and I stand there and say, "No, this has got to be a five-star record." I have to be the arbiter of that taste.

One of the things I try to stress to people is that I try to keep the reissue program going and I'm also thinking about the future and the impact that every individual release I do has on the future. If I do a best of somebody, I want it to be a best of, and I'll worry about the nooks and crannies somewhere else.

Goldmine Annual: Would Buddy Holly be a good example of that? You've had a lot of people pushing for *The Complete Buddy Holly* to be transferred to CD, but you've said you're not ready to do that because it's not really complete yet. Is that why you put out the 50-song collection just recently?

Andy McKaie: That's a good example. Buddy Holly is a legal nightmare that's been going on as long as I've been doing this job. It's finally winding its way down and it looks good for '94. Hopefully there won't be a last-minute snag. But the double CD I just put out evades all that nightmare; it doesn't deal with any of those things. Those are all tracks that we own the rights to. The legal end of it is a major pain.

Goldmine Annual: What are some of the other legal problems you face?

Andy McKaie: There are artists who won't let their songs appear on a compilation with other artists. During Elvis Presley's lifetime that never happened. The recent deal they cut with the estate changed that. I have a lot of artists that won't allow their tracks on compilations. You have to know that going in because they may be the linchpin to a compilation. There are other acts that are overexploited too.

Multi-artist compilations are a pain. Rhino is the king of the kingpins right now. They've done a very good job becoming that. They became known for that, like we did with Chess. We're lucky to have cut a niche for ourselves with that so that whatever we do on Chess gets more attention on every level than most other companies have with other reissue programs. It's because of our reputation, and Rhino has built that reputation up for multi-artist packages. They were able to sell those things.

Most of the record companies don't do that many of them because it's very difficult. The bins tend to be nightmares and it's also the first thing that doesn't get reordered.

Goldmine: There's so much of that stuff and the quality releases get mixed in with all the crap. You can look through the compilation bins and find some nine-song CD of remakes right next to a great Rhino compilation and there's no way for the uninformed consumer to tell that there's a vast difference between the two.

Andy McKaie: I mentioned a compilation before called *Classic Soul*. I've gotten letters from people who read your magazine, who actually adore that package. It's one of my favorites that I've done too. It starts in the '60s and ends in the '80s and it's 18 tracks. I'm real pleased with it but it didn't sell. It got great attention and one of the high-end magazines said the tracks on there sounded better than they did on the Rhino stuff. I don't know if that's true, but it did sound good.

The blues stuff sells, because multi-artist blues packages have their own section in the stores. Sometimes there's even a Chess section. The Duke-Peacock compilations didn't sell. Bobby Bland sold, O.V. Wright sold. It's difficult out there right now because you don't know what's good and what's bad. And there's so much of it. I think if a Duke-Peacock compilation came out four years ago it would've made a major splash.

Goldmine Annual: Do you think there's overkill going on in the reissue segment?

Andy McKaie: Absolutely there's overkill. It's been overkill for a long time. Unless you're someone like Rhino, because they're geared up to sell all this stuff. They'll do a better job than the majors because none of us are geared to sell just this stuff. So I have to put out stuff that will sell itself. That's not to take anything away from MCA, because MCA, over the years, has supported me increasingly well. They've advertised everything, they've even worked singles off my packages. They do giveaways. But this is not their main business. Their main business is to make new records and put them out, whereas Rhino, this is their main business.

Goldmine Annual: There are very few people at the major labels who are conversant in music history. You're the exception because you are well-versed in different styles and periods. Most of the people that we come into contact with have a very narrow view.

Andy McKaie: I put all the music into perspective, current as well as past. I take it with a respect. People tend to dismiss genres and I think that's horseshit. I think every genre of music has a place. In one week recently, we met over Buddy Holly, Ready For The World, Pat Boone, Bing Crosby and Nanci Griffith. That's the way it should be. We should be feeding all the different tastes. We never know which will be the next Willie Dixon or Brady Bunch and will sell, for whatever reasons, a lot more than you think it's going to sell.

Louis Armstrong's *What A Wonderful World* album is over 800,000 copies. When my son was four, about four years ago, we were in a record store and they had a small section of vinyl records in alphabetical order, so Louis Armstrong was up front. And he picked it up and ran over to me and shouted, "Daddy, your record's here!"

And the thing is it was such a hit that it was there with Led Zeppelin, Michael Jackson. It caught on and it was the right song, the right package and it sold so well we haven't done a greatest hits. It's still selling.

Most things you can assume what they're going to do. We're going to do a Frogman Henry package and I was talking to the head of distribution and he said, "I don't know what to tell you on this," and I said, "I don't either."

If you keep a reissue campaign going, if you keep it productive, and if you deal with all the elements of it, and if you approach it from some sort of intelligent base, you'll get to everything.

Goldmine Annual: Before we were discussing the process of putting together a reissue. After you locate the multi-tracks, what happens next?

Andy McKaie: You go through all the tapes and pick the one you think is the right master. Sometimes I'll pick two and I'll tell the engineer to make a final decision based on sound quality and which is the better master to use. I make sure I've got the right takes though. Then I have it sent to the studio and as soon as the engineer is available we sit down and talk about everything from using Sonic Solutions to what kind of sound I'd like to hear for this act. Then we go. I rarely sit in. I did with the Elton John box. We did the entire Elton John box EQ'ing over a Labor Day weekend, because it was overdue.

But generally I leave an engineer to his job and he leaves me a DAT reference and a cassette reference and I play the DAT in my office and the cassette in my car and send the cassette off to whoever is writing the liner notes. Then I come back to the engineer and say, "You've got the wrong tape," or, "There should be more bass on this." Generally, the producers we hire are good, like Bill Inglot.

Goldmine Annual: What does a reissue producer such as Bill Inglot actually do?

Andy McKaie: He's a great tape researcher, great researcher of sounds in general. He'll figure out the right version for you.

Goldmine Annual: What happens during the mastering phase?

Andy McKaie: You transfer it to digital, then you EQ it. EQ'ing is a process of adding and subtracting sound; to equalize the sound to make it sound the way you think it should. Some of the Buddy Holly original masters recorded in Clovis, for example, are very heavy on the bass. You have to cut back on the bass because that's not the way it should sound. When they put it out as a single, it didn't have this monstrous bottom. You trim it

down and maybe add a little on the top. You can only do so much because the basic sound is there.

Goldmine Annual: You almost have to put yourself in the shoes of someone in 1958 and try to recreate what they were doing.

Andy McKaie: You try to make it sound the way it should sound at that moment. You try to make it sound as good as it sounded, the right sound, so that the guitar comes shimmering through at the right time. But you want it to sound even better, if you can. Eventually, digital will get better as the number of digital samplings gets bigger.

The Sonny Boy Williamson comp has eight remixed tracks in stereo, but Inglot and I spent hours balancing the thing to sound like the mono and then into stereo, so you don't lose anything. You get the same sound except that it's in stereo. That's not something I do on a regular basis. I just did it with that because many people that would buy that already have the monos. But there they were, the four-track tapes, and I thought it was kind of cool and relatively easy to give people a different perspective on Sonny Boy.

Mastering is a subjective and yet not so subjective thing. There are people who are extremely good at it and people who are mediocre at it. I am not an engineer but I do have an idea of what I want in sound and I try to communicate that to the engineer.

Goldmine Annual: What is Sonic Solutions?

Andy McKaie: The Sonic Solutions system is a lot more complicated and a lot more effective than anybody thinks it is. We use it more for editing and EQ'ing than we do for the de-noising effect. As opposed to CEDAR and a couple of the others it's actually a tremendous editing and EQ bay. It's a computerized system that can do a lot of different things for your music. You can do some really interesting editing.

Goldmine Annual: So the old days of splicing tape with a razor blade are long gone?

Andy McKaie: Yeah, but I do it because I deal with analog every day. Generally, you don't do that when you go to the mastering process. Bill Inglot works on 30 i.p.s. tape until he gets into the studio. Every tape determines what needs to be done to it. The engineer and the producer have to do whatever they can to make it the best-sounding thing they can. Sometimes you get a bad source and there's nothing you can do about it. There's no highs and no lows, it's all in the middle.

Goldmine Annual: At what point do you give in and admit you've taken it as far as you can?

Andy McKaie: You have to make that judgment. You keep going until you find the best thing possible. But generally there's a point where you realize you've run out of sources. I look around the world for sources. For Tommy Roe we went to Germany and England because the tapes left over here weren't very good. We don't physically go there but I contact them— I've gotten tapes from England, Japan, Germany, France.

Goldmine Annual: How do you know where to look?

Andy McKaie: You go where you have to go. You just keep looking. I then play every tape. I'm not one of those people who orders tapes and has them sent to the studio. I'm working on a second volume of Bobby Bland and listening to everything and I'm finding songs mismarked, wrong titles. I have to sit with discographies and figure out what the title is.

When I did the first volume [*I Pity The Fool: The Duke Recordings, Vol. One*], there were five different songs marked "Sometime Tomorrow." Not different versions, but different songs.

One of them *was* "Sometime Tomorrow." Most of them contained the words "sometime tomorrow." That's why the engineers have to be a little more together too; they have a tendency to be very lazy and mark things wrong without thinking. You've got to think and you've got to ask and look if you're going to put one of these out. I would've had some very interesting responses if I'd just gone by what it said on the box.

I take for granted the fact that I'm going to be dealing with yesterday's mistakes. I've learned that over the years. I've used the wrong take, but never the wrong song. I've seen people use the wrong song. I try to be methodical.

Goldmine Annual: Do the reissue producers at the various labels compete with each other or do you see yourselves as trying to do the same thing and help each other out?

Andy McKaie: When we first started playing with packaging we were competitive and trying to make better packages than the other guy did. But we've all gotten over that. At this juncture I'd just like to make mine as good as I like to make mine. It irritates me when they're not, when I see a spelling mistake in the liner notes or I think I've put too much or too little bass in something. I think there are labels that don't do good work, and that irritates me because they own some good music and I'd like it to sound good. There are also some labels that overspend. I'm sure I've spent too much here and there but generally I watch what I spend very closely. My art department does too. We don't go overboard. Ultimately, what reissues should be to a record company is profits. Some things are costly. If you're going to do a 100-song Bing Crosby and most of it is from the pre-tape era, you're going to spend a lot cleaning it up.

Goldmine Annual: It would seem to be very difficult for a record company to lose money on reissues.

Andy McKaie: They've done it, because of overkill. Things like pull-out color spreads.

Goldmine Annual: How important is the packaging, the graphics end?

Andy McKaie: I think it has to be attractive and interesting. You can go overboard. Granted, ultimately it boils down to one thing and that's the music.

The Top 100 Most Valuable U.S. Albums From Goldmine's Price Guide to Collectible Record Albums

by Neal Umphred

The list of albums below is taken from the recently published third edition of *Goldmine's Price Guide To Collectible Record Albums.* Readers of this article need note that this book does not cover all fields of collectible records. For instance, jazz records are absent from the book though they are covered in a companion volume, *Goldmine's Price Guide To Collectible Jazz Albums,* published in 1992. Had the list below included jazz albums, one title from the book would have certainly made the grade: Dial LP-1, *The Bird Blows The Blues,* a "Limited Mail Order Edition" issued in the first half of 1949. Ads in leading trade journals of the time proclaimed this 12" album to be "The First Long Playing Jazz Record" with "14 sides/40 minutes in all."

Selling for an outrageously high price of $5.00, the album was actually panned in the July 29, 1949 edition of *downbeat* for manipulating the consumer because "there is no complete previous record [i.e., both sides of the 78 single] on the LP. Thus, you can't replace present records in your collection with the LP." At the very least this would indicate that review copies made it out. One would assume that some collectors would have purchased the first jazz album especially by the highly collectible Charlie Parker. Yet there are no copies known at this time in the hands of current collectors, making this the Holy Grail of jazz LP collectors. During the research for the jazz price guide, at least one dealer claimed that should a clean copy turn up it would fetch at least $5,000 from the Japanese market.

Which brings up another point: There are literally scores of rare jazz albums that sell to Japanese collectors for more than $1,000 in Near Mint condition that are not listed as such in the book. As one dealer noted concerning these titles, he only offers lesser condition copies to his American clientele because he knows they would balk at paying four figures for a NM copy.

Similarly, neither soundtracks (unless they feature an otherwise listed artist) nor classical albums are included in this list. Certainly, there are rarities from each genre that would easily bump titles listed below off the lower end of the list. This would include select classical titles from the late '50s on RCA Victor's "Living Stereo" maroon label with the "shaded dog" as well as Mercury's now legendary "Living Presence Stereo" releases from the same era. Likewise, a number of soundtracks would leap into the upper realms of the top 100; the privately pressed *Caine Mutiny* would certainly make the top 10!

Also, the list covers U.S. manufactured albums exclusively. Were we to take into consideration albums issued elsewhere the list would change dramatically, including several psychedelic albums (such as Bent Wind's *Sussex,* a $4,000 album from Canada, and the British *Dark Around The Edges,* currently valued at £1,800 [approximately $2,700] in *Record Collectors' Rare Record Price Guide*) and a handful of preposterously rare Elvis albums from the '50s.

Which then brings up a record that has received an incredible amount of attention lately, the red vinyl copy of RCA Victor LOC-1035, *Elvis' Christmas Album.* This piece was pressed in 1957 by a pressing plant employee at the end of the day when he squeezed some red vinyl into the press, surreptitiously manufacturing a personal collectible. The genesis of this record places it in the twilight zone of collectibles: While it is not quite a bootleg neither is it a legitimate, authorized pressing. Thus its appeal is limited to certain collectors. (For example, Perry Cox refuses to list such items in *The Beatles Price Guide For American Records.*) The employee recently sold the record for a reported $2,400 to a trio of entrepreneurs in New Jersey who have offered the record for sale to the highest bidder. At this time, the album remains unsold, though the owners have turned down a legitimate offer of $7,500.

1. **BOB DYLAN**
Columbia CS-8786 *(S)* **The Freewheelin' Bob Dylan** *1963* **20,000.00 ***
(Original pressings contain four songs—"Talking John Birch Blues," "Let Me Die In My Footsteps," "Rocks And Gravel" and "Gamblin' Willie's Dead Man's Hand"—deleted from all subsequent pressings and replaced by four new tracks, "Masters Of War," "Talkin' World War III Blues," "Girl From North Country" and "Bob Dylan's Dream." This second version remained in print as a stereo album through the '80s. For more information on the this album refer to the article "The World's Most Valuable Album" in this book.)

2. **BOB DYLAN**
Columbia CL-1986 *(M)* **The Freewheelin' Bob Dylan** *1963* **10,000.00 ***
(This is the mono version of the album above. It is important to note that while the stereo album above lists the deleted tracks on the label, no mono copy containing the deleted tracks have been found with the labels listing those tracks. That is, mono copies of this album have first pressing records with second pressing labels. Therefore, to determine whether or not you have a copy of this album, you must listen to it. . . The second version remained in print as a mono album through 1968, undergoing several label changes, which currently

Bob Dylan

The Beatles

command $25-40. "While Freewheelin' is a better album over all with the replacement tracks, it's a shame that 'Footstep' and 'Birch' couldn't have stayed. They would have added to the album's post-war/pre-Armaggedon paranoia. Also, the topicality of this album could just as easily have fit in the Reagan-Bush years as it did the early '60s. . ." — NU)

3. **THE BEATLES**
Vee Jay LPS-1085 *(S)* **The Beatles And Frank Ifield On Stage** *(Portrait cover)* *1964* **9,000.00 ***
(The front cover is a full-color painting of the Fab Four. Original pressings were titled "Jolly What! The Beatles And Frank Ifield On Stage" on the front cover and featured a cartoon of an eccentric British chap. These are worth less than 1/10 of the portrait cover version. The mono version of this album is worth $3,000 and is listed below.)

4a. **THE BEATLES**
Vee Jay SR-1062 *(S)* **Introducing The Beatles** *(Ad back)* *1963* **8,000.00 ***
(First pressing with "Love Me Do" and "P.S. I Love You." The back cover features ads for 25 other Vee Jay albums. The mono version of this album is worth $3,000 and is listed below.)

4b. **THE BEATLES**
Vee Jay PRO-202 *(DJ)* **Hear The Beatles Tell All** *(White label promo)* *1964* **8,000.00 ***
(Interviews with the Mop Tops from 1964. The stock mono copies are worth $150 while "stereo" copies were issued by Vee Jay International in 1979 and are worth $15.)

5a. **THE BEATLES**
Capitol ST-2553 *(S)* **Yesterday And Today** *(Butcher cover)* *1966* **7,500.00 ***
(Throughout the first few years of the Beatles' American career, Capitol was paring the original EMI/Parlophone albums down from 14 tracks to eleven for U.S. consumption, butchering the group's work and its intent. The left-overs were used to compile "new" albums, none of which, for the most part, have counterparts anywhere else in the world. As a means of protest, this album sported a cover photo of the four Fabs in doctor smocks cheekily handling dismembered baby-doll parts and slabs of raw meat. . . After initial copies were distributed the album was withdrawn and a new cover with a shot off four nattily attired but docile lads posing with a steamer trunk was adapted. Hirelings were paid to remove the original cover and affix the new one but, as they were paid by the piece, many took to merely pasting the second, "trunk" cover over the "butcher cover." Copies of the album with the original cover never having had a second cover pasted on to it are referred to as "first state butchers." Copies with both covers—i.e., the original cover and the second cover pasted on it—are referred to as "second state butchers." The mono version of this album is worth $3,000 and is listed below.)

5b. **THE ROLLING STONES**
London LL-3402 *(M)* **12 X 5** *(Blue vinyl)* *1966* **7,500.00 ***
(One copy of The Stones' second American long-player was found in 1989 on blue vinyl. Its official original remains a mystery although the record, graded "Poor" by the seller, immediately sold for $2,000.)

5c. **IKE & TINA TURNER**
Philles PHLPS-4011 *(S)* **River Deep-Mountain High** *1966* **7,500.00 ***
("River Deep-Mountain High" the single, often cited by both fans and critics as one of the genre's greatest achievements, was viewed as an event at the time of its release by both producer Phil Spector, his admirers and his detractors. After it failed to even dent the top 40, Uncle Phil blamed his "enemies" for the failure. And he could be right; it's almost impossible to hear this amazing single and not think "Hit Record!" After AM stations torpedoed the next single, the album was pressed in minute quantities, apparently without Spector's knowledge, to gain access to the stereo-only FM radio stations. No covers are known to have been completed. This was eventually issued by A&M in 1969. "Rockaway Records sold a copy I graded "Poor" for $2,000 in 1991." — GJ)

5d. **BILLY WARD & THE DOMINOES**
Federal 295-94 (10") *(M)* **Billy Ward & His Dominoes** *1955* **7,500.00 ***
(The Dominoes were one of the most important of the early groups, marked by strong leads with great harmonies on highly influential material. Out of their ranks rose both Clyde McPhatter (and thus, The Drifters) and Jackie Wilson.. "The first R&B group LP. . . Mint copies are all but non-existent and could conceivably command $15,000 or more." — NF)

6. **THE BEATLES**
Apple SO-385 *(S)* **Hey Jude/The Beatles Again** *(Alternate cover)* *1970* **6,000.00 ***
(Alternate cover prototypes were designed for this album when it bore the working title "The Beatles Again." Several graphic variations—including one cover with the front and back cover photos switched—are known to exist and the suggested value refers to any of the variations. The value is entirely for the cover, with or without the record inside.)

Prince

David Bowie

7a. BOB DYLAN
Columbia PC-33235 (DJ) **Blood On The Tracks** *(Original test pressing)* 1975 **5,000.00 ***
(Original test pressings—issued in plain cardboard jackets—feature alternate takes of five songs of "Tangled Up In Blue," "If You See Her Say Hello," "You're A Big Girl Now," "Idiot Wind" and "Lily, Rosemary And The Jack Of Hearts." A copy graded VG+ fetched $5,000 in 1991. "Another case where Dylan's instincts are spot on. While the original versions all have something to offer, this is a better album for the often sloppy but genuinely inspired replacement versions." — NU)

7b. PRINCE
Warner Bros. 25677DJ (DJ) **The Black Album** *(2 LP promo)* 1987 **5,000.00 ***
(This promotional version of Prince's withdrawn [by the artist] album is actually two 12" records that play at 45 RPM. There are two known copies in the hands of collectors, one of which, graded VG+, sold for $6,000 during the first weeks of 1993. This set contains the entire contents of the regular album, which is valued as $4,000 and listed below.)

8a. FRANK BALLARD
Phillips Inter.1985 (M) **Rhythm-Blues Party** 1962 **4,500.00 ***
("Copies of this album in collectible condition are so rare that delineating a price for condition is ludicrous. There are probably fewer than ten copies known to exist." — NF)

8b. THE MIDNIGHTERS
Federal 295-90 (10") (M) **The Midnighters: Their Greatest Hits** 1955 **4,500.00 ***
(The first long-player by this classic R&B ensemble. "Near Mint copies of this album are almost non-existent and are seldom for sale. A truly mint copy of this LP has not been available in years." — NF)

9a. BOYD BENNETT
King 395-594 (M) **Boyd Bennett** 1956 **4,000.00 ***
(King is noted for having released hundreds of LPs of rhythm & blues and country music in the '50s and '60s, many of which received print runs of less than 5,000. If the album sold, more were run off. If not, it was forgotten. This is one of the rarest—and most desirable—of all the Kings.)

9b. DAVID BOWIE
RCA Victor CPL1-0576 (S) **Diamond Dogs** *(Genitais cover)* 1974 **4,000.00 ***
(The cover, a painting of a dog with Bowie's head, clearly shows the canine's genitals. . . at rest. Prior to release the Bowiedog was effectively neutered by an airbrush. These "dickless" covers are as common as hen's beaks. The value here is entirely for the cover, with or without the record inside.. "Once only rumored to exist and then only as a slick not affixed to the cardboard, there are now four known copies, the two most recent sold for $4,000 and $6,000." — NF)

9c. CHARLES BROWN
Aladdin 702 (10") (M) **Mood Music** *(Red vinyl)* 1952 **4,000.00 ***
(This classic by the legendary Brown—who is still doing personal appearances—is arguably the rarest of the rare Aladdin 10" albums. The black vinyl version is listed at $2,500 below.)

9d. AMOS MILBURN
Aladdin 704 (10") (M) **Rockin' The Boogie** *(Red vinyl)* 1954 **4,000.00 ***
(This was Amos' first LP; his last was recorded for Motown when he was past his prime and released in 1963. The black vinyl version of this album is listed at $2,500 below.)

9e. PRINCE
Warner Bros. 25677 *(S)* The Black Album *1987* 4,000.00 *
(This is the version prepared for commercial release in 1987 but pulled by Prince. A sealed copy sold in 1990 for $5,000. The two-LP promo version of this album is valued at $5,000 and listed above.)

10a. THE FENDERMEN
Soma MG-1240 *(M)* Mule Skinner Blues *(Blue vinyl)* *1960* 3,500.00 *
(Long rumored to exist—as have other colors—a copy of this album on blue vinyl turned up in 1992 and was promptly sold for $4,000. . . Copies on both non-opaque black vinyl-valued at $2,000—and normal opaque black vinyl—$1,250—are listed below.)

10b. JACK KEROUAC
Dot DLP-3154 *(M)* Poetry For The Beat Generation *1959* 3,500.00 *
(Preposterously rare collection withdrawn by Dot and issued on their Hanover subsidiary, which is also rare and currently commands $300. The value assigned is based on the assumption that this album would attract the attention of literary aficionados as well as record collectors.)

11a. THE BACHS
Raio *(No number)* *(S)* Out Of The Bachs *1967* 3,000.00 *
(Recently unearthed punk/pysch gem. A VG copy sold for $2,000 prior to the discovery of a small cache of sealed copies, three of which have reportedly sold for $5,000 each. "Minor key, haunting and melodic... like an American Zombies if they were in a garage/psych mood." —NS)

11b. THE BEATLES
Vee Jay LP-1062 *(M)* Introducing The Beatles *(Ad back)* *1963* 3,000.00
(First pressing with "Love Me Do" and "P.S. I Love You." The back cover features ads for 25 other Vee Jay albums. The stereo version of this album is worth $8,000 and is listed above.)

11c. THE BEATLES
Vee Jay SR-1062 *(S)* Introducing The Beatles *(Blank back)* *1963* 3,000.00
(First pressing with "Love Me Do" and "P.S. I Love You." The back cover is completely blank, devoid of any printing. Long rumored to be a promo it is now assumed to be a mis-pressing. The mono version is worth $1,200 and is listed below.)

11d. THE BEATLES
Vee Jay LP-1085 *(M)* The Beatles And Frank Ifield On Stage *(Portrait cover)* *1964* 3,000.00
(The front cover is a full-color painting of the Fab Four. Original pressings were titled "Jolly What! The Beatles And Frank Ifield On Stage" on the front cover and featured a cartoon of an eccentric British chap. These are worth less than 1/10 of the portrait cover version. The stereo version of this album is worth $9,000 and is listed above.)

Frank Sinatra

The Rolling Stones

11e. THE BEATLES
Capitol T-2553 *(M)* **Yesterday And Today** *(Butcher cover)* *1966* **3,000.00**
(First-state mono "butcher cover." Refer to the first-state stereo butcher "Yesterday And Today," listed above at $8,000, for the full story on this rarity.)

11f. JOHNNY BURNETTE & THE ROCK 'N' ROLL TRIO
Coral CRL-57080 *(M)* **Johnny Burnette & The Rock 'N' Roll Trio** *1956* **3,000.00 ***
(The "trio" in the title is deceptive: This is really Johnny Burnette with brother Dorsey and Paul Burlison. Along with RCA Victor LPM-1254, Elvis Presley, *this is one of the first—and definitive—rockabilly albums. "Most copies fall into the VG or less grading, selling for $200-500. Mint copies are virtually unknown and would command prices in the $5,000-10,000 range." — NF)*

11g. DAMON
Ankh 968 *(S)* **Song Of A Gypsy** *(Gatefold cover)* *1970* **3,000.00**
(Original versions of this privately pressed psych album have gatefold covers with both an Egyptian ankh and the title embossed on the front. Reissues with a standard single-pocket cover are listed below at $1,500)

11h. AMOS MILBURN / WYNONIE HARRIS / CROWN PRINCE WATERFORD
Aladdin 703 (10") *(M)* **Party After Hours** *(Red vinyl)* *1954* **3,000.00 ***
(This r&b collection features three of Aladdin's favorite artists; while Milburn rated an album of his own, Aladdin 704, Rockin' The Boogie *(also on this list), neither Harris nor Waterford saw their work on LP other than collections such as this. The black vinyl version of this album is listed below at $2,000.)*

11i. THE ROLLING STONES
London NPS-3 *(DJ)* **Through The Past, Darkly** *(Picture disc)* *1969* **3,000.00 ***
(Prototypes for a rejected picture disc back in '69. Two variations are known: one has the cover from "High Tide & Green Grass" on both sides the other has "High Tide" backed with Ten Years After's "Sssh." The value is entirely for the record whether or not it includes a cover.)

11j. FRANK SINATRA
Reprise FS-1028 *(S)* **Sinatra-Jobim** *(Test pressing)* *1969* **3,000.00 ***
(This album, a follow-up to 1967's successful "Francis Albert Sinatra And Antonio Carlos Jobim," [Reprise 1021] was cancelled after test pressings were made. I assigned this record the the widest suggested range in the book, $1,000-5,000, due to both the lack of knowledge concerning its rarity and the utter unpredictability of Sinatra collectors. Company notes show that 3,500 copies were manu-factured as 8-track tapes and all but three ordered destroyed. . . Issued in a plain cardboard jacket.)

12a. THE BEATLES
United Artists UAL-3366 *(DJ)* **A Hard Day's Night** *(White label promo)* *1964* **2,500.00 ***
(This is the white label promo edition of the commercially released album to the Fab Four's first feature film. Exactly why this promo is so rare is unknown; this movie was heavily promoted by U.A. as producers of both the film and the soundtrack. . .)

12b. THE BEATLES
Apple KAL-1004 *(DJ)* **Yellow Submarine** *(Radio spots)* *1968* **2,500.00 ***
(While this film is, of course, forever linked with John, Paul, George & Ringo, the group had nothing to do with the film in any way, 'cepting the contribution of a few unreleased songs. This album contains a series of brief "spots," or plugs, intended for radio broadcast to promote the animated film. Issued in a plain cardboard jacket.)

12c. CHARLES BROWN
Aladdin 702 (10") *(M)* **Mood Music** *(Black vinyl)* *1952* **2,500.00 ***
(The red vinyl version of this album is listed at $4,000 above.)

12d. FRANK FROST & THE NIGHTHAWKS
Phillips Inter.1975 *(M)* **Hey Boss Man!** *1961* **2,500.00 ***
(Supposedly there were only 500 copies of this LP pressed. In 1975 a noted West Coast collector found 490 odd covers without records. "There are probably less than 10 complete copies in the hands of collectors today." — NF)

12e. JEFFERSON AIRPLANE
RCA Victor LPM-3584 *(M)* **Jefferson Airplane Takes Off!** *1966* **2,500.00 ***
(Original mono pressings contain "Runnin' 'Round This World" and alternate takes of both "Go To Her" and "Let Me In," whose lyrics make allusions to sex or LSD. These three were deleted from all subsequent pressings. The latter two were replaced by cleaned up versions while "Runnin'" sat on the shelf until it was gathered onto the "Early Flight" album five years later. Stereo copies with these tracks are not known to exist.)

12f. PAUL & LINDA McCARTNEY
Apple MAS-3375 *(DJ)* **Ram** *(Mono promo)* *1971* **2,500.00 ***
(The label does not identify this as a promotional release but it clearly states that the album in "Monaural." In most cases it was was shipped to radio stations in the same cover as the regular stereo version, sometimes the two LPs were side by side in the same jacket.)

12g. AMOS MILBURN
Aladdin 704 (10") *(M)* **Rockin' The Boogie** *(Black vinyl)* *1954* **2,500.00 ***
(The red vinyl version of this album is listed at $$4,000 above.)

12h. GATEMOUTH MOORE
King 684 *(M)* **Gatemouth Moore Sings The Blues** *1960* **2,500.00 ***
(This album, Moore's sole release of the '50s and '60s, has been erroneously titled in previous editions of this book as I'm A Fool To Care. *"One of the legendary King albums; only a few have survived the past four decades. A Near Mint copy recently sold for $3,000." — NF)*

13a. LLOYD GLENN
Swing Time 1901 (10") *(M)* **Lloyd Glenn** *1952* **2,250.00 ***
("There are probably less than 10 copies in the hands of collectors. One sold for $2,750 in 1991." — NF.)

13b. THE INDEX
D. C. *(No number)* *(M)* **The Index** *1968* **2,250.00 ***
(The price is for original record in an original cover, both featuring "New York Mining Disaster." Most copies have the original record in a second pressing cover which lists "Fire Eyes." These are worth $1,500 in Near Mint condition. Second pressings with"Fire Eyes" are worth $1,200. "Along with Tom Rapp's Yetti-Men, this is one of the missing links between surf and psych." — NS)

Jackson Browne

14a. THE BEATLES
Vee Jay SR-1062 *(S)* **Introducing The Beatles** *1964* **2,000.00**
(Second pressings with "Please Please Me" and "Ask Me Why." There are three known label variations for this title, each with the same approximate value. The mono versions are worth $200-400 depending on the label.)

14b. THE BEATLES
Vee Jay VJS-1092 *(S)* **Songs, Pictures And Stories Of The Fabulous Beatles** *1964* **2,000.00**
(Issued in a nifty gatefold cover where the front flap is only 8" across. This album contains second pressings of Vee Jay 1062, Introducing The Beatles with "Please Please Me" and "Ask Me Why." There are three known label variations for this title, each currently carrying the same approximate value. The mono version of this album, which has been heavily counterfeited, is worth only $300.)

14c. THE BEATLES
Vee Jay DXS-30 *(S)* **The Beatles Vs. The Four Seasons** *1964* **2,000.00**
(This double-album collects Vee Jay 1062, "Introducing The Beatles," with 1065, "The Golden Hits Of The Four Seasons." It was issued with a fold-open, full-color poster of the Liverpudlians, worth an additional $300 in Near Mint condition. The mono version of this album is worth $500. Beatles collectors seeking to piece together the most perfect set of this album—cover plus the two discs—have driven the value of The Four Seasons album up beyond what a Seasons' collector would normally value the album at!)

14d. THE BEATLES
United Artists Help-Show *(DJ)* **Help!** *(One-sided, open-end interview)* *1965* **2,000.00**
(This one-sided disc should not be confused with the more common [sic] two-sided interview album, valued at $1,500 and listed below. Issued in a plain cardboard jacket.)

14e. THE BEATLES
Capitol ST-2553 *(S)* **Yesterday And Today** *(2nd state butcher cover)* *1966* **2,000.00**
(For the story on this title, refer to the listing for the "first-state stereo" listed above at $7,500. This is the second-state "butcher cover" with the "trunk" cover pasted over the original "butcher" cover. Second-state monos are worth $600.)

14f. BRIGADE
Band'n Vocal BVRS-1066 *(S)* **Last Laugh** *1970* **2,000.00** *
(Privately pressed album from a NW group. "Highly over-rated album with a couple of high points, including a psychedelic Doorsish number." — NS)

14g. JACKSON BROWNE
(No label) *(S)* **"Jackson Browne's First Album"** *1967* **2,000.00** *
(This double-album is the Holy Grail for Jackson's fan. Actually, this is an untitled publishers demo intended to get other, established artists to record the his songs. None of these recordings have been released to the public. Issued in a plain cardboard jacket.)

14h. THE FENDERMEN
Soma MG-1240 *(M)* **Mule Skinner Blues** *(Non-opaque black vinyl)* *1960* **2,000.00** *
(Copies exist on a non-opaque black vinyl that allows light to shine through with a reddish tinge when held up to a light source. Normal opaque black vinyl copies are worth $1,250 and are listed below while a few copies are known on colored vinyl and, valued at $3,500, are listed above.)

14i. THE FIVE ROYALES
Apollo LP-488 *(M)* **The Rockin' Five Royales** *(Green label)* *1956* **2,000.00** *
("Later pressings with yellow labels are either second pressings issued in the '60s or repros from the early '70s. Copies with a purple label are known to exist but would seem to be later pressings done to confuse the collector." — NF)

14j. FRACTION
Angelus WR-5005 *(S)* **Moon Blood** *197?* **2,000.00**
(This privately pressed psychedelic collectible was issued in a cover with a die-cut "window" to allow the moon on the inner sleeve to show through.)

14k. JOHN LENNON & YOKO ONO
Nautilus NR-47 *(S)* **Double Fantasy** *(Alternate cover)* *1980* **2,000.00** *
(Alternate cover prototype has bright yellow strokes added to the background and a red heart drawn on Yoko's bosom. There is one known copy and it is not for sale. The estimate is for the cover alone and based wholly on assumption. . .)

14l. LITTLE ESTHER [PHILLIPS]
King 622 (M) **Down Memory Lane With Little Esther** 1959 **2,000.00 ***
("Among the best R&B albums ever made, this masterpiece is high on everyone's want-list. A Mint copy would command a price in the $3,000-4,000 range." — NF)

14m. MARIANI
Sonobeat 1001 (M) **Perpetuum Mobile** 196? **2,000.00 ***

14n. AMOS MILBURN / WYNONIE HARRIS / CROWN PRINCE WATERFORD
Aladdin 703 (10") (M) **Party After Hours** *(Black vinyl)* 1954 **2,000.00**
(The red vinyl version of this album is listed above at $3,000.)

14o. PHAPHNER
Dragon LP-101 (S) **Overdrive** 197? **2,000.00**
("People are finally deciding this privately pressed psych album is a really good record as well as a really rare record. . . after they have all disappeared." — AJ.)

14p. ELVIS PRESLEY
RCA Victor *(No number)* (S) **International Hotel Presents Elvis, 1969** 1969 **2,000.00 ***
(Complimentary boxed set supposedly limited to 2,000 copies presented to the hotel's dinner guests for Elvis' first show of the year. The box contains a copy of LPM-4088, "Elvis," a copy of LSP-4155, "From Elvis In Memphis;" a 1969 Elvis Record & Tape Catalog; a 1969 Elvis wallet calendar; an 8 x 10 full color photo; two 8 x 10 black & white photos; and a letter of introduction and thanks from Elvis, Colonel Parker and RCA. Note that approximately 80% of the value is for the box alone.)

14q. ELVIS PRESLEY
RCA Victor *(No number)* (S) **International Hotel Presents Elvis, 1970** 1970 **2,000.00 ***
(Complimentary boxed set supposedly limited to 2,000 copies presented to the hotel's dinner guests for Elvis' first show of the year. The box contains a copy of LSP-6020, "From Memphis To Vegas / From Vegas To Memphis;" a copy of 47-9791, "Kentucky Rain" / "My Little Friend" with picture sleeve; a 1970 Elvis Record & Tape Catalog; a 1970 Elvis wallet calendar; a photo booklet; an 8 x 10 black & white photo; a hotel menu with Elvis on the front; and a letter of introduction and thanks from Elvis, Colonel Parker and RCA. Note that approximately 80% of the value is for the box alone.)

14r. ELVIS PRESLEY
RCA Victor VPSX-6089 (Q) **Aloha From Hawaii Via Satellite** 1973 **2,000.00**
(Van Camp, the sponsors of Elvis' 1973 CBS TV Special, acquired stock copies of the album and affixed stickers to the cover with their Chicken Of The Sea tuna maid noting the TV special. A single sheet with a picture of Elvis and a description of the show was included and these LPs were distributed to members of the corporate office.)

14s. THE ROLLING STONES
London NP-1 (DJ) **High Tide & Green Grass** *(Alternate cover)* 1966 **2,000.00 ***
(This rejected cover prototype has the same graphics as the released version except title on the front is on two lines [the released version has the title on three lines] and in radically different type. One copy is known to exist. The value is for the cover alone.)

14t. VARIOUS ARTISTS
Tamla TM-222 (M) **The Great Gospel Stars** 1961 **2,000.00 ***
("This is by far the rarest LP on any Motown related label; there are only a few copies known to exist. A Mint copy sold for $3,000 in 1991." —NF)

14u. VARIOUS ARTISTS
Warner Bros. *(No #)* (DJ) **Jamboree** *(Soundtrack)* 1955 **2,000.00 ***
(This soundtrack contains snippets of songs by a potpourri of artists of the time and was shipped out to radio stations. It is one of the rarest albums of the rock 'n roll era and sells for $300-500 in VG or less condition.)

14v. WEST COAST POP ART EXPERIMENTAL BAND
Fifo M101 (M) **West Coast Pop Art Experimental Band** 1966 **2,000.00 ***
(A privately pressed psych album from a group that later recorded several fine albums for Reprise. Copies of this album recently turned up without covers and quickly sold out. . .)

15a. THE MUSIC EMPORIUM
Sentinal 69001 (S) **The Music Emporium** 1969 **1,750.00**
(Privately pressed psych LP is one of the classics of its genre. "Typifies West Coast acid/psych with some nice raga type songs." — NS)

15b. VARIOUS ARTISTS
(No label) (DJ) **Carnival Rock** *(Soundtrack)* 1956 **1,750.00 ***
(Sampler from the movie of the same name pressed on red vinyl and shipped to radio stations in a plain cardboard or paper sleeve.)

15c. VARIOUS ARTISTS
DCA Prod. *(No number)* (DJ) **Rock, Rock, Rock** *(Soundtrack)* 1956 **1,750.00 ***
(Publisher's demo disc intended for inclusion in the soundtrack for the movie of the same name.)

16a. LONNIE JOHNSON
King 395-520 (M) **Lonesome Road** 1958 **1,600.00 ***
("One of the most sought-after LPs on King. Mint copies are impossible to find and would fetch prices in excess of $2,500." — NF)

16b. BIG JAY McNEELY
Federal 295-96 (10") (M) **Big Jay McNeely** 1954 **1,600.00 ***
(Primarily a major R&B session man given a shot at solo success by Federal and King.)

16c. THE MIDNIGHTERS
Federal 395-541 *(M)* **The Midnighters: Their Greatest Hits** *1955* **1,600.00 ***
(This is the 12" repackage of the 10" version, 295-90, valued at $4,000 and listed above. "Very rare in collectible condition and generally sold in VG or less for $100-200." — NF)

16d. THE PENGUINS
Dootone DTL-204 *(M)* **Best In Rhythm 'N Blues** *(Red vinyl)* *1957* **1,600.00 ***
(Although this is a various artists album with the second side containing tracks by The Dootones, Meadowlarks and Medallions, as all of side one is by The Penguins this is generally considered their first album by collectors. Black vinyl reissues are worth $150.)

17a. THE BEATLES
United Artists Help-Int. *(DJ)* **Help!** *(Open-end interview)* *1965* **1,500.00**
(This two-sided disc should not be confused with the rarer one-sided interview album, valued at $2,000 and listed above. Issued in a plain cardboard jacket.)

17b. ROY BROWN / WYNONIE HARRIS / EDDIE VINSON
King 668 *(M)* **Battle Of The Blues, Volume 4** *1960* **1,500.00**
(This various artists compilation features tracks by each of the three R&B giants. "One of the rarest and most sought-after numbers on King. A recent auction of a NM copy had several bids in excess of $1,500." — NF)

17c. C. A. QUINTET
Candy Floss 7764 *(M)* **A Trip Through Hell** *1969* **1,500.00**
(A legendary private pressing psychedelic album. "While this psych classic is not a mega-rarity—copies do turn up for sale—it virtually never shows up in truly Near Mint condition." — AJ)

17d. THE CHAMPS
Challenge CHL-601 *(M)* **Go Champs Go** *(Blue vinyl)* *1958* **1,500.00 ***
(Regular black vinyl copies of this album are worth $250.)

17e. THE CRYSTALS
Philles DT-90722 *(E)* **Twist Uptown** *1963* **1,500.00**
(This is the electronically rechanneled—using Capitol's patented "Duophonic" system—version from the Capitol Record Club.)

17f. DAMON
Ankh 968 *(S)* **Song Of A Gypsy** *(Standard cover)* *1970* **1,500.00**
(A private pressing from the garage/psych '60s/'70s. Original versions with gatefold covers are listed above at $3,000)

17g. DION & THE BELMONTS
Laurie LLPS-2002 *(S)* **Presenting Dion & The Belmonts** *1959* **1,500.00 ***
("A few copies of this album exist in stereo although they have been grossly overlooked by collectors." — NF. Mono versions of this album are worth $100.)

17h. BOB DYLAN
Columbia CL-1986 *(DJ)* **The Freewheelin' Bob Dylan** *(White label promo)* *1963* **1,500.00 ***
(For the story on this title, refer to the first listing of this list. This white label promo plays the second version with "Masters Of War," etc., but the front cover has a DJ title & timing strip listing the deleted tracks, including "Talkin' John Birch Blues.")

17i. THE EBON-KNIGHTS
Stepheny MF-401 *(M)* **First Date With The Ebon-Knights** *1963* **1,500.00**
(Early soul group from the Chicago-based Stepheny label.)

17j. THE FIVE KEYS
Aladdin 806 *(M)* **The Best Of The Five Keys** *(Maroon label)* *1956* **1,500.00**
(Contrary to previously published listings, legitimate blue label pressings of this album do not exist. "Truly Mint copies of this marvelous group LP are virtually impossible to find and would command prices in the $2,000-3,000 range." — NF)

17k. THE FUGITIVES
Hideout 1001 *(M)* **The Fugitives At Dave's Hideout** *1968* **1,500.00**
(Privately pressed album contains punkish covers of current hits. "There are less than five copies known to exist." — NF)

17l. GRANMA'S ROCKERS
Fredlo 6727 *(M)* **Homemade Apple Pie** *1967* **1,500.00**
(A private pressing from the garage/psych '60s/'70s.)

17m. HAYMARKET SQUARE
Chaparral 201 *(S)* **Magic Lantern** *1969* **1,500.00**
(After the first batch of this [privately pressed psych] album disappeared there have been no copies for sale in years." — AJ)

17n. THE JACKS
RPM LRP-3006 *(M)* **Jumpin' With The Jacks** *1956* **1,500.00**
("Mint copies of this extremely rare LP are unheard of. . . Prices in the $2,000-3,000 range would be readily forthcoming if one were found." —NF)

17o. AMOS MILBURN
Motown 608 *(M)* **Return Of The Blues Boss** *1963* **1,500.00 ***
(Subtitled "The Return Of Amos Milburn," this is one of the rarest of all Motown collectibles.)

17p. ELVIS PRESLEY
RCA Victor AFL1-2428 (S) **Moody Blue** *(Multi-colored vinyl)* *1977* **1,500.00**
(Three variations are known of this colored vinyl prototype: purple-on-white, red-on-white and yellow-on-white. The price is for the record alone. "This album—Elvis' last release prior to his death—was mediocre even by the less than inspiring standards he had been setting for himself the previous half-dozen years." — NU)

17q. LULA REED
King 604 (M) **Blue And Moody** *1959* **1,500.00**
("Mint copies of this album are extremely rare commanding prices in excess of $2,000." — NF)

17r. THE SHAGS
Third World 3001 (S) **Philosophy Of The World** *1970* **1,500.00** *
(This legendary piece of ultimate anti-commercialism, recorded by a trio of sisters under the guidance of their father, moved noted avant garde composer Carla Bley to remark "They bring my mind to a complete halt." This was eventually issued on Rounder and is worth $10.)

17s. VARIOUS ARTISTS
Celebrity 1000 (M) **World Famous Rhythm And Blues** *1959* **1,500.00**
(Perhaps the most valuable generally distributed commercial compilation of great group records from the '50s.)

17t. VARIOUS ARTISTS
RCA Victor SP-33-66 (DJ) **Christmas Programming From RCA Victor** *1959* **1,500.00**
(This special seasonal sampler features one Elvis track and was issued in a full-color paper jacket with photos of the artists, including EP. Counterfeits of the sleeve exist but are black & white reproductions.)

18a. THE ROLLING STONES
London LL-3375 (DJ) **The Rolling Stones** *(White label promo)* *1964* **1,400.00** *
(This is the only white label promo Stones album until 1971's "Sticky Fingers.")

18b. VARIOUS ARTISTS
(No label) (DJ) **Go, Johnny, Go** *(Soundtrack)* *1959* **1,400.00** *
(Sent out to radio stations in a plain cardboard jacket. Copies were handed out at the movie's premiere in a deluxe box that also included a a lobby card and a "press pass" to the showing. The box is preposterously rare with no reasonable way to suggest a value.)

19a. THE FIVE SATINS
Ember ELP-100 (M) **The Five Satins Sing** *(Blue vinyl)* *1957* **1,300.00** *
("The blue vinyl pressing of this album is a second pressing with the multi-color Ember label in the second jacket. It was probably pressed in a semi-authorized manner. However, it is extremely rare." — NF)

19b. JIM REEVES
Abbott LP-5001 (M) **Jim Reeves Sings** *1956* **1,300.00** *
("Probably the rarest C&W album. . . I've never seen a copy." — JG)

20a. THE BEATLES
Savage BM-69 (M) **The Savage Young Beatles** *(Yellow label)* *1964* **1,250.00** *
(This album collects material recorded by Tony Sheridan in Hamburg in 1961 and features John, Paul, George and Pete Best as The Beat Brothers on four tracks. This pressing has a yellow label and was issued in a jacket with a glossy orange cover. This album exists with an orange label and yellow jacket, valued at $100, that has been reproduced.)

20b. THE FENDERMEN
Soma MG-1240 (M) **Mule Skinner Blues** *(Opaque black vinyl)* *1960* **1,250.00** *
(This is the regular black vinyl pressing; copies exist pressed on non-opaque black vinyl. Valued at $2,000 it is listed above, as is a colored vinyl version, listed at $3,500.)

20c. THE NEW TWEEDY BROTHERS
Ridon 234 (S) **The New Tweedy Brothers** *196?* **1,250.00** *
(Classic private pressing from a Portland psych group originally issued in an oversized, hexagonal cover. "Although they're from Portland they sound more like a Bay Area group with a tremeloed guitar sound ala John Cipollina." — NS)

20d. THE ROLLING STONES
Abkco MPD-1 (DJ) **Songs Of The Rolling Stones** *(Orange cover)* *1975* **1,250.00** *
(This collection of song snippets has an orange-tinted photo taken from the group's aborted TV Special, "The Rolling Stones' Rock & Roll Circus." Another version of this album has an inset shot of the group in a country field setting and is worth $300.)

21a. THE BEATLES
Vee Jay LP-1062 (M) **Introducing The Beatles** *(Blank back)* *1963* **1,200.00**
(First pressing with "Love Me Do" and "P.S. I Love You." The back cover is completely blank, devoid of any printing. Long rumored to be a promo pressing it is now assumed to be a mis-pressing. The stereo version is worth $3,000 and is listed above.)

21b. THE BEATLES
United Artists SP-2359 (DJ) **A Hard Day's Night** *(Open-end interview)* *1964* **1,200.00**
(Issued in a plain cardboard jacket.)

21c. BOLDER DAMN
Hit HRI-5061 (S) **Mourning** *1971* **1,200.00**
(Another privately pressed collectible from the early '70s.)

Buddy Holly & the Crickets

The Marvelettes

21d. BUDDY HOLLY & THE CRICKETS
Decca DL-8707 (M) That'll Be The Day *(Black & silver label)* *1958* **1,200.00**
(This album was reissued with a black label and a rainbow color spectrum through the center that is worth $250.)

21e. INDEX
D. C. *(No number)* (M) The Index *1968* **1,200.00**
(Later copies of this privately pressed album feature "Fire Eyes." Original pressings with "New York Mining Disaster" are worth $2,000 and are listed above.)

21f. THE MARVELETTES
Tamla 229 (M) The Marvelettes Sing The Hits Of '62 *1962* **1,200.00**
(Original covers have a large "M" with a '62" inside a circle. Later pressing covers are basically black with each of the song titles inside white circles and are worth $500.)

21g. THE PATRON SAINTS
(No label) (M) Fohhoh Bohob *1969* **1,200.00**
(A legendary psych album pressed up by the band for local distribution.)

21h. ELVIS PRESLEY
RCA Victor LPM-1382 (M) Elvis *1956* **1,200.00**
(Black label with "Long Play" on the bottom. Some later pressings contain an alternate take of "Old Shep." The matrix number in the trail-off vinyl ends with either "17S" or "19S.")

21i. SHANNON, DEL
Big Top 12-3003 (S) Runaway *1961* **1,200.00**
("This legendary stereo album was never even listed in the Schwann catalog! Apparently the stereo masters were cut without Del's knowledge [as sales of stereo albums meant a higher royalty to the artist]. When Del was shown a copy at the Bottom Line in 1980, he was totally surprised." — NF)

21j. BILLY WARD & THE DOMINOES
Federal 395-548 (M) Billy Ward & His Dominoes *1956* **1,200.00**
(This is a 12" reissue of the 10" album valued at $7,500 and listed above.)

21k. BILLY WARD & THE DOMINOES
Federal 395-559 (M) Clyde McPhatter With Billy Ward & His Dominoes *1957* **1,200.00**
(This album collects sides featuring Clyde McPhatter prior to his formation of The Drifters.)

How To Run A Fan Club and Maintain Your Sanity

by Stephen Thompson

Engines of Aggression is a year-old industrial rock group with a new EP out on Priority Records, and one of many things the label is doing to promote the band is establish a fan club.

Of course, with just six songs and a smattering of college radio airplay to its credit, not many people have rushed to add themselves to the organization's legions. But Kira Matlow, a Priority publicist working to establish the fan club, said it's still a matter of time.

"Right now we're just setting up a list of names and taking it from there," Matlow said. "It's pretty hard to just set up a fan club from scratch, but once we get some more interest we can start doing promotions."

"We're trying to compile lists of people who like the band so we can keep them posted on what's going on," she added. "We're desperately trying to get listed in publications' fan club listings, but it's really hard to do because they're such a new band."

Matlow's trials are fairly simple compared to those facing most fledgling fan clubs and their presidents. The Engines of Aggression Fan Club has full support of the artists and, of course, the band's label. This club is designed primarily to serve as a mailing list to build grass roots support, rather than a full-fledged fan club that charges dues to its members. And perhaps most importantly, the club's budget comes directly out of Priority's ample coffers.

But many of Matlow's struggles are shared by just about every fan club president in existence. How do you build interest? How do you publicize your fan club without losing your shirt? And finally, how do you run a fan club and maintain your sanity?

Linda Kay, president of the National Association of Fan Clubs, spends much of her time helping fan club presidents answer those questions. And while steering clear of the roadblocks certainly isn't easy, Kay said most are avoidable if you're aware of what you're getting yourself into.

"The first thing anyone starting a fan club needs to do is think about it a lot," Kay said, "because it's a major commitment and a lot of people don't really understand what it's going to entail.

"It involves a lot of work, it sometimes entails a lot of money, and you don't make any money," Kay said. "Very rarely do fan clubs ever make money.

"Most people really think we're making a killing out there," she continued. "Most of the time we're losing money, and we're lucky if we're breaking even. You could ask just about any fan club president and that's what he or she will tell you. There's got to be a genuine sense of commitment, because it's a lot of hard work."

So if there's no money in it—and there really isn't—why bother?

"The benefit of running a fan club is getting to meet people from all over the world who you never would have gotten to meet," Kay said. "All my best friends I've gotten through fan clubs. Some people want to start a fan club thinking that's going to get them closer to a celebrity, and sometimes that happens, but it's very rare.

"You should start a fan club because you like the celebrity and you want to be in contact with other people who like that celebrity," she said. "You want to be able to collect and trade, and you want to do something special for his or her fans."

But it's difficult to run an organization as complicated and time-consuming as a fan club and still make a living, especially when you're footing the bill for the bulk of the club's expenses.

"It's really just a hobby," Kay said. "There are a few people who make a living at it, but that usually involves running more than one fan club. I've been trying to start a fan club business for some time, and it is really, really hard."

So thinking the process through will undoubtedly prevent nightmares and dashed expectations for the unprepared. But more steps must be followed to insure your sanity, not the least of which is actually seeking permission from the celebrity's management.

"If you don't get permission, the worst thing in the world is to get a letter telling you to cease and desist, and that happens," Kay said, adding that sometimes celebrities switch to uncooperative management companies, making matters unsettlingly unpredictable.

The third and final major step, of course, is to think about your budget. Before laying out huge quantities of cash on printing and merchandise and advertising, think about the number of people your club will reach and play your hand conservatively.

Until recently, Kay was president of a club for fans of the long-running TV show "Perfect Strangers," and membership never grew to more than 50 or so members. And the recruitment problem isn't necessarily due to lack of interest, but lack of advertising resources.

For music-related fan clubs it's not so bad, since many fan clubs can put their addresses in CD sleeves, hand out flyers at music conventions or take out fairly cheap advertising in any number of music papers. For television fans, those outlets aren't there.

But no matter where your interest lies, promotions aren't cheap, and you should expect to start your club on an embarrassingly small scale. Keep that scale in mind when you start thinking about merchandising.

No matter how cheaply and efficiently you run your club, some problems will come out of nowhere. The Root Boy Slim Fan Club has operated for years, enjoying constant dedication and support from the artist. But early in summer 1993, the 48-year-old singer died, leaving his fan club in a difficult position. The club can continue as a means of remembering the celebrity's gift, but for obvious reasons, its members can never again enjoy support from the artist or the artist's management.

Some fan clubs thrive following the artist's death—witness the dozens if not hundreds of Elvis fan clubs—but others go belly up because of shifts in the commercial tides. When musicians even temporarily stop producing hits, fan clubs can lose the momentum and attention they need to survive.

Parody artist "Weird Al" Yankovic's fan club, the Close Personal Friends Of Al, was dissolved several years ago following the box office failure of his movie *UHF* and the poor sales of the film's soundtrack.

But Yankovic is a venerable performer with a supportive record label, and he's managed to stage several successful comebacks since the fan club disbanded. As of this writing, Yankovic's career is on yet another upswing (an album will be out soon), but there is still no replacement for the Close Personal Friends Of Al.

On the other hand, some fan clubs continue to thrive despite the fact that their celebrity hasn't enjoyed national popularity in years. (Witness the aforementioned Root Boy Slim Fan Club.) Kay said that more than anything else, this depends on who's in charge of the club.

"It really hinges on the devotion of the person running the club," Kay said. "They're talent really, because clubs can stay successful as long as they can keep it interesting. But it's very hard to run a fan club when there's no current news."

It may seem difficult to believe, but in many ways it's actually easier for a fan club to deal with a decline in popularity than the opposite: How would you cope if your cozy little fan club was suddenly inundated with hundreds or even thousands of new members?

Maggie McManus, who operates the quarterly *Monkee Business Fanzine,* endured that success and saw her newsletter's circulation surging from 400 to a whopping 11,000 in less than a year during the height of the Monkees' 1986 comeback. According to McManus, what started as a part-time hobby soon became a full-time chore.

"I didn't eat and I didn't sleep," said McManus, who still operates the club with about 1,600 members. "I was working full-time already and also putting on a Monkees convention, so it got really hairy. From the moment I came home at night I would start working on the mail, and I'd work straight through midnight or one in the morning. Then I'd get up early, go to work and start all over again."

"Our address was on the Monkees' tour program, so as soon as they went on tour it started," she continued. "The day after their first concert we went to the mailbox and there were like a hundred letters from the place where they had played. It continued like that all year, averaging about 300 letters a day."

And while McManus's workload increased, the amount of personal care she could give to each fan decreased.

"We had to set priorities," McManus said. "People who were looking for information on how to join the fan club got processed first, and next were people who were actually sending money to join the fan club or were ordering back issues. People asking questions about the band had to wait, and a lot things never got a personal answer, but they got answered in the magazine itself."

And since the primary purpose of most fan clubs is to serve as a pen pal network and a breeding ground for friendships, it's difficult to justify running such a massive, comparatively impersonal operation. (The money helped.) In the years following the Monkees comeback, McManus has been able to return to a less frenetic schedule—with more time to devote to individual fans—but the club's relatively brief period of financial prosperity ended as well.

"We came out ahead for a while and spent a lot of the profits on taxes," McManus said. "We left the remaining money in the fan club account, and in the last few lean years when we've been losing money, that money's been there as a cushion. No fan club makes money for long."

Beyond that notoriously common financial drain, another key frustration fan club presidents often face is the infuriatingly ill-conceived stereotypes that surround their operations.

"When people think of fan clubs, they think of fanatics who run around shooting people," Kay said. "There's also this frustrating misconception that they're all a bunch of screaming teens, but most fan club presidents I've met are surprisingly normal. You simply can't run a business like this and keep everybody happy and put out good materials without being sane."

In fact, fan clubs are one of the most rational, sane ways of expressing appreciation of a celebrity's work. But fan clubs should always be prepared for the possibility of an individual fan going a bit overboard: In the early '80s, McManus was nearly run over by a berserk fan who felt angry and alienated by her (the fan's) inability to get close to one of the Monkees.

As with any personal or professional endeavor, the operation of a fan club brings about countless possibilities for sanity-straining situations to arise (a fact that should be pretty apparent by now). But there are also ways fan club presidents can derive numerous benefits from their positions, and the rewards of running a fan club usually outweigh the pitfalls. The following are 15 relatively surefire suggestions designed to make your life easier:

1. **Take advantage of your opportunities.** If you run a music-related fan club, pass out flyers at conventions. If there are publications that print free fan club listings (like *Goldmine*), don't pass up your chance. Send out press releases to your hometown newspapers, which love printing features on what makes the community unique. ("Can you believe there's a national Archies fan club right here in Beaver County?") Don't scoff at free publicity—you never know who could be reading, and you can't lose.

2. **Trade ads with other fanzines.** If there are other fan clubs whose audience might be interested in your celebrity, try to work out a mutually beneficial deal where you promote each others' outfit. Again, there's absolutely no cost, and you could make some new friends—not to mention new members—in the bargain.

3. **Network, network, network.** Why learn from your own mistakes when you could learn from other people's mistakes? Talk to people who've been there before, and find out what works and what doesn't. Just keep in mind that each club is unique, and that there are very few ideas that work for everyone.

4. **If you can afford it, advertise in publications that offer cheap rates.** The publications most widely utilized by fan clubs are Kay's *Fan Club Monitor,* which will connect you with other fan club presidents, and (of course) *Goldmine,* which has proven successful for numerous music-oriented clubs.

5. **Join the National Association of Fan Clubs.** More ideas can be gleaned from a single issue of the quarterly *Fan Club Monitor* than you'll find just about anyplace else, and it's the most efficient way to communicate with other people who are experiencing the same trials and joys you are. (See #3.) Your club will also be put in the NAFC's database, meaning that any-

one inquiring about your celebrity will be given your organization's address. Club memberships are $12 a year, individual memberships cost $10 a year and "The Fan Club Guide"-- which should tell you just about everything else you need to know about starting and running a fan club—costs $5. (See address below.)

6. **Seek out other available listings.** *The Who's Who Directory* and *The Directory of Organizations* are both widely read and examined by fans looking for clubs to join. Take advantage of these; you can find them in your local library.

7. **Always cooperate with the wishes of the celebrity.** Don't give out private or personal information if you've been lucky enough to obtain it. You'd just as soon stay on the celebrity's good side, and you can really mess up his or her life by leaking secrets. You don't do anyone a favor by doing this.

8.**Be frugal.** Countless fan clubs have died painful premature deaths as a result of excessive postage and printing costs; see if you can arrange bulk mailings and shop around for the best printing deals. Particularly in large markets, printers have to price themselves competitively to survive. Take advantage of this. When taking overseas orders, get an international money order in U.S. funds (or you'll spend more cashing the check than it's worth), and always try to buy production supplies in bulk.

9. **If you don't have access to a computer, get access.** McManus vowed never to write out another address label after doing 1,000 of them for an issue of *Monkee Business* Fanzine. You don't quite realize how convenient computers are until you have to do a big job manually. Anything you can do to make operations more efficient is a godsend.

10. **Other fan clubs are your friends—not your competitors, and certainly not your enemies.** If your favorite celebrity has multiple fan clubs, these can be valuable resources rather than a detriment. Different clubs often offer different features, and there's no reason you can't all work together. (This doesn't always work, but that's no reason not to try.) It's frustrating when new clubs seem to pop up every day looking to take a bite out of your audience—there were more than a hundred Monkees fan clubs by the end of 1986—but you all share a common (and noble) goal.

11. **Sure, you'll lose money, but never overcharge for anything.** According to Kay, "The fastest way to go out of business is to overcharge. Fans have a way of letting you know if they're not happy." Remember that you're in this for the fans' benefit—they deserve the best possible product for their money.

12. **Try merchandising, but always take advance orders.** Merchandising can rescue you from financial ruin, but you have to be careful. Test your market before laying out money, and get your payment upfront. That way you won't get hurt.

13. **Don't lose sight of reality.** It's difficult to start any fan club, so don't expect your organization to blossom into a lucrative empire overnight. There are businesses that actually make money running multiple clubs at one time, but these companies have more time, connections and financial backing than you do right now.

14. **Always stick to your production schedule.** According to McManus, "That's the biggest pet peeve I hear from people about other fan clubs. The least you can do for your subscribers is make the effort and come out on time, even if you don't have a great deal of material to put in a given issue."

15. **Listen to your members.** Not only do they pay the bills, as the cliche goes, but they also know better than anyone what to put in a desirable product. In the end, they're the most important beneficiary of your efforts. Give them what they deserve.

There's no way to prepare yourself for every difficulty that crops up when you're running a fan club, but there's no excuse for venturing into the business blindly. Take the proper precautions, don't overspend, and be sure to communicate with others as much as possible. You'll enjoy your hobby more, and you'll undoubtedly develop friendships that last a lifetime. What could be more rewarding than that?

Engines of Aggression Fan Club, c/o Priority Records, 6430 Sunset Blvd., Hollywood, CA 90028, Attn: Rock & Alternative Division.

Monkee Business Fanzine, 2770 South Broad St., Trenton, NJ 08610, Attn: Maggie McManus.

The National Association of Fan Clubs, P.O. Box 7487, Burbank, CA 91510-7487, Attn: Linda Kay, Phone: 818-763-3280, FAX: 818-752-4848.

Root Boy Slim Fan Club, 3834 Sheffield Circle, Danville, CA 94506, Attn: Duane Straub, Phone: 510-736-1480, FAX: 510-736-7844.

"Everyone Needs It When It's New!"

An Overview Of Collectible CDs '93

by Neal Umphred

In 1992 Capitol stunned the jazz world by announcing the deletion of more than 40 CD titles from its Blue Note catalog. Originally an independent label (the owners sold their interest to Liberty Records in 1966), Blue Note stands as a testimony to how record companies could be run: Every aspect of the recording process, record making and artist handling was done with class, consideration and painstaking attention to detail. Hence, Blue Note produced not only the finest jazz records of the '50s but arguably the most important body of work of any label in any genre at any time.

When aficionados heard that select titles by such stalwarts as Art Blakey, Kenny Burrell and Paul Chambers were to be relegated to the cut-out bins, pandemonium ensued. Those collectors not lucky enough to find the deleted titles for $5.99-7.99 are now seeking those they missed (and the number of deleted titles currently exceeds 90). One desperate collector recently ran an ad in *Goldmine* offering $75 for a particular title he could not locate! For the active collector of CDs, the next few years may be a crossroads: Those items that have proven elusive the past few years may be all but impossible in the next few.

"Verve, EmArcy and Pacific Jazz seem to be disappearing as well [as Blue Note]," noted Armand Lewis, a long-time collector of jazz on vinyl who has picked up the CD bug and collects both mediums. "Every time I go to the store I notice something that used to be there is gone. I bought many of the titles as they were released and sought out the deleted titles as cut-outs as they were announced and still haven't been able to find some discs, such as Sonny Clarke's *Sonny's Crib* and Joe Henderson's *In And Out.* In the jazz world, catalog titles—especially the reissues—seem to stay in print two or three years and then quietly disappear.

"Minor jazz artists on major labels are also hard to find. Even such quality product as RCA's Novus series and Island's Antilles label, both noted for breaking new artists and giving a shot to established names that have failed to achieve real prominence, are hard to find. I have no trouble selling the Blue Notes with the sawmark in the box for $15-20 per disc. A lot of titles I am just holding on to for now, speculating on the future of CDs as collectibles."

The First Collectible Compact Disc

In the beginning, shortly after God said "Let there be CDs," there came to be a small but avaricious following for the new digital wonders here in the United States. Since there were almost no facilities to manufacture this product, a good percentage of the selection of titles available were imported from elsewhere, particularly Japan and West Germany. (Yes, readers, once again the captains of American industry floundered in their decision-making and were profitably beaten to the punch.) While some titles made it to the retail racks with seeming abandon, others snuck in—occasionally on dubious legal or technical grounds—and were gone almost overnight, creating a demand for them as collectibles.

For example, when the Beatles' *Abbey Road* was issued by EMI/Odeon in Japan, it also arrived in shops around the country as a fairly high-priced import ($25-30 was the norm). After it was determined that the disc had been manufactured without the requisite authorization from the main company in England, it was discontinued. Because of this, it is often thought of as the first truly collectible compact disc, selling for $100 or more ... back in 1983!

It is imperative that at this point American readers understand that, like rare records, CDs have an international market open to them. And, in the case of some items, the main market is the disc's country of origin, where it is [obviously] more of a collectible there than here. While the aforementioned *Abbey Road* is a desirable item in the U.S., it is one of the most collectible of all discs in Japan, *especially* in light of the fact that the bulk of the press run for this title was exported. Gary Johnson of Rockaway Records of Los Angeles, CA, recently attended one of the world's largest record collectors conventions in Japan as a dealer. He brought with him four copies of *Abbey Road* and sold them all immediately at $500 a piece and was told that he had underpriced them for the Japanese market. Even more remarkable is the fact that original pressings of the disc featured an "obi," a paper wrapper around the display box that bore Japanese characters. Copies still in the box with this obi are valued at $1,000!

Another highly sought-after Japanese pressing is the EMI/Toshiba pressing of The Beach Boys' *Pet Sounds.* In 1987, when the company released the disc with two bonus tracks, both the lack of a U.S. version of this now legendary album *and* the extra minutes of music caused a sensation. When the disc was pulled for reasons similar to the*Abby Road* affair (Capitol of America poo-pooed its early release as the company was still in protracted negotiations with the group), this, too, started bringing $100 from American collectors. Shortly afterwards, it was announced that Capitol would issue the same disc with the extra music. Here in the States demand died, but not so in Japan, where it now commands $200-250.

The liner notes for RCA's *Jefferson Airplane Loves You* boxed set which boasts better audio fidelity than previous Jefferson Airplane reissues

Promotional CDs

Long-time vinyl collectors would assume that the most sought-after CD *should be* the out-of-print "original," just as it is with records. It is the disc that was pressed and made available to the public that should carry the most demand from the most collectors in the long run. This is especially true with CDs since some titles have been kept in print long enough to, in major league parlance, "catch a cuppa coffee" and then pulled. Thus far it is this type of disc that has caught the *least* attention. Titles that were initially issued in the early to mid-'80s using LP masters and then pulled and replaced with digitally remastered version have yet to really catch the attention they deserve as artifacts *not* as examples of aesthetics or ethics.

Abbey Road and *Pet Sounds* stand in opposition to a trend that has been going on in record and CD collecting circles since the early '80s: The tendency for collectors of contemporary artists to pay excessive amounts of money for newly manufactured items, especially those of a promotional nature. That is, just as Springsteen collectors were willing to pay $20-25 for each of the Boss's 12" promo singles upon release, only to see the price drop with the immediate appetite of the diehards assuaged, CD collectors may find themselves paying more for an item than the item's (eventual real) market value simply for the pleasure of having it.

This is part of the "I must have it now" phenomenon to which collectors in all fields are prone (merely glance at the heated sports card market of the past decade where collectors too young to drive are spending several dollars to purchase a brand new card). Another perspective on this often baffling behavior comes from Gary Johnson, who aptly—and perhaps more kindly—noted "Everyone needs it when it's new!"

Many of the better known examples have also gone through the roof upon release only to float back to the floor when the immediacy of the devout collectors' needs have been met. When George Harrison's *Cloud Nine* was sent out to radio stations in 1987 as a limited edition with a "picture" of Harrison's profile against a cloudy sky silk-screened on the disc, collectors went ga-ga and sent the price of this new item spiraling. Within a short time the fever-pitch sent the disc up over the $100 mark as the "I must have it now" attitude dulled the senses of his fans. Soon, however, the realization that the demand was greater than the supply attracted almost as much attention as the disc and the price plummeted back to earth.

In 1988 when Sire was determined to break Brian Wilson's solo album as big as possible, at least three separate CDs were shipped out to anxious programmers for consideration. Aside from a special promotional pressing of the album, a disc titled *Words And Music* which included selections from the album punctuated with Brian chatting was pressed. A second item was

NEW

FRAME THE UNFRAMABLE

Swingframe™

FRAME, REMOVE AND CHANGE VALUED RECORD ALBUMS *IN SECONDS*–

EVEN WHILE THE FRAME IS ON THE WALL!

CUSTOM METAL FRAME
MUSEUM QUALITY ARCHIVAL
ULTRAVIOLET PROTECTION

Swing-Open,
Place Record,
Swing-Close–It's that simple!

CALL OR WRITE FOR INFORMATION

SWING FRAME

10 BUCKMINSTER ROAD, ROCKVILLE CENTRE, NY 11570
TEL: (516) 678-7772 FAX: (516) 678-0907

Absolutely the Best Selections of Import Compact Discs Available Anywhere

WORLDWIDE CD

P.O. Box 543-G, Villa Park IL 60181
Phone 708-941-7619
FAX 708-941-7923

Goldmine CUSTOMER SERVICE

Send $1.00 for Catalog

EUROPE
England
France
Germany
Italy
Spain

ASIA
Japan
Korea

N. AMERICA
United States
Canada

CD BANZAI!™

DIGITAL MUSIC EXCHANGE

MAIL ORDER

If it exists on Compact Disc, we'll find it! We have direct connections. Let us find the CDs you're looking for. Collector items and laser discs, too. We mail anywhere!

Call for a free list of your favorite live artists on CD Complete catalog of over 3,500 titles available for $7.50 + $2.50 handling. And receive a 10% off your first order from the list.

CALL 24 HOURS A DAY

Phone 213-965-1103 • FAX 213-653-2311

CD BANZAI

P.O. Box 17081
Beverly Hills, CA 90209-2081

WRITE TO RECEIVE A FREE SAMPLE COPY

ICE

The Monthly CD Newsletter

Comprehensive and cutting-edge compact disc news for consumers and collectors.

ICE provides collectors and enthusiasts with a monthly dose of unrivaled CD coverage. Each issue is crammed with exhaustive release schedules and the first word on new albums, upcoming box sets, reissues and industry news. Add to that coverage of special collector's issues, promotional discs, imports, European live discs, and the CD Watchdog column — which allows readers a dialogue with record label executives, who scramble to explain mistakes — and you have *ICE* covering CDs like no other publication.

•"*ICE* is probably the best source for CD news in the world . . ." — *New Musical Express*

•"When *ICE* arrives . . . every month, there's always a fight to see who reads it first, and there are few higher recommendations than that." — *Billboard*

•"*ICE* isn't afraid to name names of poor-value discs, or single out the praiseworthy ones." — *Musician*

•"*ICE* digs up scoops and raises issues . . . and is passionate, opinionated, frisky and fun." — *Los Angeles Times*

For a complimentary copy of *ICE*, just drop us a line; overseas customers please remit two IRCs. First class subscriptions are $30/one year or $54/two years in North America; for overseas airmail, $40/one year or $75/two years (U.S.funds only please). Send check, money order or credit card info (Visa or Mastercard number and expiration date) to:

Goldmine CUSTOMER SERVICE

ICE, P.O. Box 3043-M, Santa Monica, CA 90408 U.S.A.
Or fax: (310) 829-2979 or call (310) 829-1291 (9-5 Pacific time, M-F)

an ersatz leather-type wallet that included a 32-page booklet with copious notes and pictures and a special disc featuring silk-screened portions of the album cover artwork. While *Words And Music* was issued on both vinyl and disc, the wallet was a CD-only edition and caught fire with the long-dormant interest of BW's followers in new collectibles, peaking at $50. All three of the aforementioned – the Harrison above and the two Wilson pieces – can be found in today's market for approximately $25 each, a more realistic value for such recent collectibles.

CD singles reading "Promotion/Demonstration Only – Not For Sale" all but glut the marketplace. Unless the title is by a highly collected artist, these singles can often be found for 50¢ to $1.99 at shows and shops. Promotional compilations are another story, as these appeal to the album-oriented collector and are generally pressed in smaller quantities and are, consequently, much, much harder to find. The Rolling Stones are responsible for two such discs: *Stones On CD* is currently valued at $100-150, a price it has maintained for several years, while the more recent *Say Ahh* goes for $50-75. But the hottest item on collectors' want-lists is a brand-spanking-new (as this is being written) comp of John Cougar Mellencamp, an item collectors' shops are getting $40-50 for.

While promotional limited editions should prove to be just that, limited in number and carrying some prestige and value with it, commercially manufactured items bearing the "limited edition" standard can mean any number of possibilities. While most are generally in the 10,000 range, American companies have been known to manufacture limited *(sic)* runs of 250,000 copies of an item perceived to be of value on the market. One recent trend has been the proliferation of supposedly limited edition promos from Japan. Many of these are unexceptional compilations advertised as "only 200 made." While there certainly are rare discs pressed in small quantities, most companies here and abroad press enough to meet the needs of the broadcast industry and those of their own representatives, who use promos as a form of reward to regional hustlers who have moved product. Customers should be wary of new items with high prices advertised this way.

Part of the promo phenomenon is the manufacturing of special syndicated radio shows. Whether in their former vinyl form of their current incarnation on compact disc, these shows are usually shipped to radio stations in plain paper sleeves with cue sheets and notes. These are much rarer than other promos, generally manufactured in lots of 500-1,500 (one show per station). While there are a variety of types of programs, the shows that either contain a complete live performance (*King Biscuit Flower Hour* series is perhaps the best known) are the most sought-after, often selling for $100 or more upon release.

Shows that concentrate on one artist's career and include interviews, commentary and album tracks are a distant second. Of course, should the show contain previously unreleased material from album projects, that would dramatically affect the value. The many shows that play hit singles, golden oldies, etc., by many artists are at the bottom of the totem pole. And for good reason: Should a collector decide to opt for everything that features a track by a popular star, he or she could spend countless dollars purchasing discs with the same [already owned] hit single(s) over and over. (For verification of this syndrome, refer to your nearest Elvis or Beatles collector.)

What About Out-Of-Print CDs?

"I don't see collectors seeking out original label CD pressings yet with nearly the gusto they've always had for LPs," noted Pete Howard, editor and publisher of the monthly CD newsletter *ICE,* and a record collector himself. "In fact, it may end up going in the opposite direction of what's happened with LPs, at least with reissues. Who's going to want RCA's David Bowie CDs when they're so vastly inferior to Rykodisc's? Only the completist, the same person who has a full set of Beatles LPs on Capitol's early '70s orange label or every incarnation of *Live At The Star-Club* that's come out. But unless you're talking about someone like the Beatles, that's probably a small group of consumers.

"It gets more interesting and unpredictable with new releases. Up to this point, I've seen almost no market for first CD pressings by contemporary artists. With the Lemonheads and Stone Roses, for example, the original CD pressings didn't contain "Mrs. Robinson" and "Fool's Gold," respectively. Therefore, only the collector would want an original pressing, since those discs have less music than the second pressings, with no other difference. At that point it gets down to collecting just for collecting's sake – which I guess we're all guilty of to some degree. But most of your high-ticket collectibles carry some value beyond just their rarity, such as unique graphics or music that's unavailable elsewhere.

"The first CD pressing of Bruce Springsteen's *Nebraska* has the extended version of 'My Father's House,' so that's highly collectible; but who cares about early pressings of his other albums? If anything, they sound worse than what you'd buy today! The aforementioned Bowie discs from RCA don't give you anything different except advertisements for Perry Como and Harry Belafonte. And sure enough, here in L.A. I've seen them gradually drop from $50 to $15 at the local swaps. Admittedly, that may have something to do with Bowie's career being as cold as ice ... but I think long-time record dealers who are automatically applying vinyl collecting standards to the new digital formats may find themselves stranded somewhere down the road."

Johnson of Rockaway Records agreed tentatively but added, "It's safe to say that select CDs will attain collectible status if they are by major, collectible artists. The original, colored disc pressings of Madonna's first album will almost certainly grow in stature and value to Madonna collectors. So will Prince. Beatles collectors are already searching out each and every variation, both in the group and solo releases. Whereas it's hard to imagine, say, the Cars' first CDs attracting a future following."

Both Howard's and Johnson's views on collectibles are currently applicable in the CD market. An example of deleted pressings commanding collectors' attention is RCA's initial venture into the digital domain with their first Elvis Presley discs in 1984. With the need for *some* releases representing the biggest money-maker in the history of entertainment, company executives in charge of Presley product lifted the masters from four of Elvis's classic '50s albums and transferred them to disc. *Elvis Presley* (PCD1-1254), *Elvis* (PCD1-1382), *Elvis' Golden Records* (PCD1-1707) and *50,000,000 Elvis Fans Can't Be Wrong: Elvis' Gold Records. Vol. 2* (PCD1-2075) reached retail racks in the latter part of the year. These first four Elvis discs have a story for collectors...

When RCA finally caved in to the stereo market in the early '60s and remastered Elvis's material into a hideous fake stereo, the normal butchering of the mono signal (splitting the signal, boosting the bass on one side, the treble on the other, etc.) was added to the already over-modulated masters. By 1969, with the (unfortunate) demise of monaural, these were all that were left for the album buyer. For the CDs, RCA simply used the available album masters and it was "electronically reprocessed stereo" versions that CD customers were treated to in 1984.

In celebration of the 50th anniversary of Elvis's birthday, RCA had mapped out 1985 as a big year, with company spokesmen announcing the deletion of the fake stereo titles and the imminent release of the four titles in "digitally restored mono." These same spokesmen made a bit of a rah about the complicated process that was used to restore Elvis to his former sonic cleanliness—with virtually no mention of the whys involved. No one was about to admit that the company had long since misplaced the original masters and had only the reprocessed stereo tapes to work with. And it was these much-doctored tapes that were once again placed in the hands of specialists, this time for some extraordinary digital surgery.

Simply, a computer was instructed to create a series of signals that were the 180 degree opposite of the extraneous noise on the masters, including the boosted bass and treble from the stereo remastering and as much of the overly generous echo as possible. This new tape was then laid over (i.e., played simultaneously) the existing master, "masking" the offending sounds. From this a new master tape was created for digitalization and transfer, and, *Voila!*, the digitally restored mono compact disc was born! The process was a modest success. While the emerging CDs were a dramatic improvement over anything that had been available for nearly two decades, they remain a pale copy of the original vinyl albums.

RCA also issued its David Bowie catalog at about the same time as the Presley discs. Unfortunately for the company, Bowie was in the process of severing relations with them and taking the rights to his works elsewhere. Thus the Bowie RCA titles were in and out of print and quickly started selling for $30-50 each, even though they were, like the Elvis titles, lifted from LP masters. Bowie finally struck a deal with Rykodisc and all of his albums were remastered and reissued with bonus tracks, dramatically affecting the demand for the RCA discs. By 1992 they had fallen into the $15-25 range, although they remain difficult to find.

Paul McCartney's Apple and Columbia catalog were initially issued domestically by Columbia. After Mac's return to Capitol in 1985 (*with* his complete roster of previous recordings), the Columbia titles were withdrawn and reissued by Capitol. Each of the original half-dozen McCartney/Wings CDs on Columbia now fetch an easy $40-50 with the double-disc *Wings Over America* valued at $100-125 (add a 10 to 15 percent premium on the first pressings that read "Made in Japan"). Probably the most sought after item is the former Fab's *oeuvre* in the American pressing of the commercial version of the "My Brave Face" CD5 single. As it followed the identical UK pressing, which had preceded it as an import into American stores, there was little demand for it from retailers. Consequently it is now the rarest domestic McCartney CD and sells for $100-125.

On a more mundane level, there are the various design permutations that various company's discs have gone through in the past few years. In the case of RCA, the company's original CDs featured a blue border around the disc and the motto "Made in Japan" on the right side. As domestic plants could not keep up with the demand—or there simply were not enough plants in the States—most discs were manufactured abroad in the first few years of the digital era. These pressings were followed by new pressings that were identical in color and design but replaced the Japan credit with "Made in U.S.A." (Other companies used both Japanese and German pressing plants and some early American discs read "Made in Germany.")

Within a few years, the blue discs were replaced with a new design: A black border with lightning like RCA in an oval on top. This design was recently altered, keeping everything but returning the basic block letter RCA in a box at the top of the disc. Thus, the completist—and you can bet that RCA counts on there being a few of them—can collect *four different pressings* of many titles by a variety of artists! Fortunately, while this gives the more obsessed collectors something to do, it has not yet reached a point where it is adversely affecting any pocketbooks. But, a word to the wise: If the need to have an "original" is part of you, search out those Japanese pressings now—-tomorrow never knows.

The Art Of Special Packaging

One aspect of the industry's recognition of collectors has been the designing of special packaging and limited editions, which long ago reached the point of overkill.

Boxed sets have been a huge profit for the companies and artists over the past few years. For some reason, consumers are willing to plunk down big bucks for a boxed set of an artist's material even though the customer is not necessarily a big fan of that particular artist. The attractiveness of the packaging, the usual inclusion of a well-made and informative booklet, the sense that one is getting everything of value by the artist—these have led to a lucrative market. Led Zeppelin's box is said to be the first to have passed the million-mark in sales, but that is a deceptive figure as the industry counts the individual discs as separate sales. The Elvis Presley box, *The Complete 50's Masters,* is near the 500,000 mark for complete boxes sold, a staggering accomplishment given that this material has been in print in various and sundry formats over the past five decades!

Now that the ecologically unnecessary long-boxes are a thing of the past, completists are searching them out. Many collectors kept them with each purchase usually collapsing them along their folds and storing them away. (When retailers began removing new discs from their long boxes and placing them in more theft-proof plastic holders, astute collectors requested that the stores collapse those of artists they collected and set them aside for their purchase.) As many discs often had two different boxes—the original box that accompanied the first issues and the less unique box that came with the second, or budget reissues, the avid collector seeking these out has a monumental task before him or her. And, it goes without saying that these have yet to be cataloged and listed anywhere for the ease of said collectors.

Attempts by the artists and industry to replace both the long-boxes and the plastic jewel boxes include the "digi-pak," where the jewel box was done away with and the disc was enclosed in a cardboard wallet-like assembly that folded neatly. These were shipped with plastic supports on each side to keep the jackets from bending. A prominent example of the digi-pack is first pressings of U2's *Achtung Baby.* Another format is the "eco-pak," which was similar to the digi-pak but without the extraneous plastic. These were issued with a sticker on the shrink-wrap advising the handler "Do not tear or discard." An example of this is Deee-Lite's *Infinity Within.* Both of these are already obsolete; completists are advised to find them while they can.

And Then There Are "Manufactured" Collectibles

Another factor contributing to the "grab it now" aspect of collecting in-print CDs is that, while the industry touted its initial product as "perfect," it has continually made new strides in the technology of the digital medium, improving on previously perfect (*sic*) product. Yet the corporations have yet to live up to their ubiquitous promises to consumers since the CD's inception that prices would come down as demand and sales went up. After the success of the Proclaimer's "I'm Gonna Be" as part of the soundtrack to *Benny & Joon*, Chrysalis raised the price of its four-year-old disc, *Sunshine On Leith,* from which the track had been lifted, from its mid-line list of $11.99 to a full $15.99!

The recent boxed set, *The Beach Boys* from Capitol improves on the sonic fidelity of the complete set of albums previously issued by the company on its highly lauded two-fer series. Similarly, RCA's *Jefferson Airplane Loves You* is a step above the digital remastering on their two-disc compilation *2400 Fulton Street*. To the audiophile-oriented Beach Boys and Airplane fan, this renders the previous discs "unfit."

The medium itself and its proclaimed abilities to provide superior sound remains a bone of contention and, one must remember, that most of the 14-bit CDs purchased during the past decade are already obsolete by the industry's new 20-bit sampling techniques. CD collectors who must have the best of each title could find themselves replacing their entire collection of 14-bit discs in favor of the 20-bit reissues as they did with their vinyl—only to find that, in another few years, the technology will again improve. Those of you asking "If they *were* perfect, how could they be improved?" will probably be asking the same question after the next technological advances force the new 20 bit discs into the cut-out bins. Nonetheless, the digital medium has been embraced by the public and has garnered a new breed of collector who will require constant input on the often errant machinations of the industry.

"Basically, the collectors of today are collecting what the labels want them to collect as opposed to what was traditionally collected by record collectors," said Dave Hyde, manager of a retail CD store and a collector himself. The industry has caught on to collectors: New titles are being issued in a variety of ways to induce collectors. For instance, some companies are issuing first pressings in brightly colored trays (that hold the disc in place in the jewel box). These trays also form a visible portion of the "spine" along the left of the jewel box's outside front and thus can be quite eye-catching, especially when placed on the wall alongside a multitude of normally black spines. George Thoroughgood's *Get A Haircut* was issued with a neon-green tray that jumped out of the displays. These special trays are then replaced with plain black ones on subsequent print runs.

Even more interesting is the packaging of discs with graphics either on the tray or in the bottom of the jewel box underneath the tray. Sonic Youth's *Dirty* was issued with a colored tray that depicted a rather amusing (or offensive, depending on your preference) couple engaged in "dirty" sexual activities. As these graphics cannot be seen unless the disc is opened (and, hopefully purchased before said opening), the interest in these collectibles are often generated by word of mouth or through collectors' publications such as *Goldmine* and *ICE* and fanzines and newsletters.

Much to the amazement of many older collectors, this has led to an increased fascination with "manufactured collectibles" (ala the picture disc phenomenon of the late '70s and early '80s), where fans are buzzing about the sundry possibilities in which the latest disc by their favorite artist has been packaged or, ahem, gimmicked up. While Beatles devotees also go bonkers—and often bankrupt—searching out picture sleeve variations, label printing errors, promotional hand-outs, ad infinitum in the same way, they are doing it after the fact.

That is, those items were manufactured in an age of virtual innocence and an almost complete lack of self-consciousness, prior to the development of record collecting as an organized hobby in the wake of the original O' Sullivan Woodside price guides by Osborne & Hamilton. (This of course does not apply to the collectors of group vocal 45s, whose world exists independent of the mainstream of vinyl collectors.) In this admittedly cynical view, the gung ho zeal with which CD collectors fall in line to pay their hard-earned money for items with no established history is not unlike the wave of collecting hysteria where Elvis fans threw their money at the never ending array of junk that permeated the market in the wake of his death in 1977. (Anybody wanna buy some Elvis whiskey decanters?)

Possibly the most outrageous—and impressive—example of the manufactured collectibles are the highly sought-after "limited edition" boxes emanating from the other side of the Atlantic. Enterprising European entrepreneurs recognize the market here and have taken to providing retailers with what can only be termed "unauthorized boxed sets." These are often sets of an artist's legitimately manufactured European CD singles collected and presented in deluxe packaging that can be both striking and quite extraordinary, from wooden boxes with metal catches to miniature coffins. Once available almost exclusively through the collectors' market (in the mail or at local shops and swaps), these are not turning up in "reputable" mainstream retail stores. These sets reside quite comfortably in legal limbo: The discs themselves are legitimate; only the packaging is not company or artist authorized. Thus far, the industry has taken little notice, much to the delight of collectors.

Two other big ticket items that fit into this scene are the picture disc CDs of *Elvis' Gold Records, Vol. 2* and *Sgt. Pepper's Lonely Heart's Club Band*, both of which originated in a shroud of mystery, occluded in controversy. Turning up in the late '80s, these attractive items were immediately collectible, due both to their vague origins and the hype surrounding them, although executives from both companies disowned them. The controversy surrounding these discs continue, as does the demand. *Even though they are bootlegs*, they are both attractive and rare and currently show up for sale with asking prices in the $200-300 range. (Those dealers who continue to maintain the discs' authenticity ask even more.)

For those pondering "What's next?," there are two schools of thought: One, that the industry will milk the physical software medium once again by introducing a smaller disc that holds considerably more music (perhaps up to two hours) with even better fidelity, or, two, that this is the end of the line for physical product. That is, that as much as the corporations will attempt to introduce new formats, the public will not accept them.

Those who argue for either side can point to the recent innovations of the DCC and the mini-disc: The former argue that this indicates the desire of the industry moguls to coerce the consumer into replacing his or her CD collection for yet another round of conspicuous consumption and that, just as with 8-tracks and cassettes, and vinyl and CDs, they will figure out a way to pull it off. The nays can point to the quick demise of those two formats as proof that the public has had it and will stick to CDs. Until, of course, the not too distant future where each home will be able to "order" the latest work by an artist on his or her computer via modem and the company with pipe the desired music down disc and bill the consumer. At which point the current crops of young CD collectors will be parents having to explain to the next generation why they remain fixated on an obsolete format...

Promotional Memorabilia

by Lisa L. Barker

Collectors who own everything there is to possibly own from favorite artists love to find the most obscure, bizarre, unique items they can find to round out their collections. Enter the world of collecting promotional memorabilia.

You have seen them throughout the pages of *Goldmine*, the Led Zeppelin "object," the Elvis Costello dart board or the Bruce Springsteen keychain. Valid collectible memorabilia, which cost the collector a pretty penny, but costs the record companies literally that ... pennies.

"On the average promotional items cost us very little to make," said a Columbia record executive, who refused to reveal his name. "Take for instance the Bruce Springsteen tennis shoe key chain we made in 1975 to promote *Born To Run*. They cost us damn near nothing to make." But the keychain alone is currently going for about $100.

Promotional memorabilia items are technically not to be considered collectors' items, at least not according to the record companies that put them out. Their "legal" sole purpose is to draw attention to an artist from radio station disc jockeys and music store mangers, in hopes they will see fit to promote that person or group extensively. But it doesn't always work that way.

Most promotional items, no matter how cute or creative, usually get tossed by those it is sent to. Others keep the unique items, while some sell them, upsetting record exces, who insist the goodies are not to be sold.

"I don't think it's right to sell a free item given to a radio station or a record store in good faith," said Capitol Records Promotional Purchasing Manager Ann Petrone.

Collectors say, possibly the first promotional item for disc jockey and music retailers was a letter opener and magnifying glass set, which came out in 1967 from Capitol Records. Both items carried a Capitol logo, with various Capitol artists on them, including the Beatles' *Sgt. Pepper's Lonely Hearts Club Band* and the Beach Boys' *Pet Sounds*. Collectors say if you can find the rarities they're worth an estimated $1000.

Record companies have been known to spend elaborate amounts of money trying to promote an artist. Take for example a clock Capitol Records made to promote M.C. Hammer's "Can't Touch This" single. The promotional piece showed the former Oakland A's batboy-turned rapper "dancing" on the clock with the title "Hammer Time". Collectors say the item is worth about $200.

Columbia came out with a similar product in 1980 to promote Rockpile's *Seconds Of Pleasure* release. The company designed an alarm clock, complete with the album cover on the face. The time piece is currently worth about $150 in mint condition.

Other elaborate pieces, or at least, unique items, have included a wine goblet and wine package from RSO Records, for the Bee Gees' 1979 release of the *Spirits Having Flown* album. The item came complete with a bottle of wine with the glass and collectors say if found intact, the item could go for about $100.

One of the less expensive items found, both to make and to buy, came from the Ohio Players. In 1978, Mercury Records issued a jar of honey to promote the album of the same name. Although unique, the piece only sells for about $10.

Promotional items also have had their share of controversy. In 1980, Polydor issued a cocaine mirror to promote Pat Travers's song "Snortin' Whiskey and Drinking Cocaine." The item was pulled from distribution after international record executives became outraged by the product. With that story, needless to say, if you can find the item, it is considered a collectible, although collectors vary on what the piece would actually sell for.

One of the most popular groups of the past twenty years to collect is KISS, but collectors say the group's promotional items leave a lot to be desired in the creativity department. Casablanca Records released cardboard hanging mobiles or wall hangings for several of the group's releases. The pieces are worth (if mint condition, which is hard to find for any paper goods) an estimated $25-150. But in the band's later years, record companies wrote off the cheaper items for substantial offerings. In 1989, PolyGram issues a pyramid-shaped paperweight to record company employees only. The piece, to promote *Hot In The Shade*, is worth about $100.

Another in-house collectible came out for the group's later releases. Record employees were treated to leather jackets promoting the group's releases. The pieces are worth about $350.

Record companies have also been known to issue only certain promotional pieces to certain areas, almost as if in an effort to find out who is selling or keeping what. Take, for example, a 1979 "beanie" hat, complete with a propeller from CBS Records, to promote Elvis Costello's *Armed Forces* album. The piece was only issued to southwestern United States representatives. Whoever currently owns the freebie could ask about $50 for it. CBS also released a whistle to promote the same album. The catch on this piece is to find both the olive green and white ones that came out. Those are worth, collectors say, about $100 a piece.

The range of promotional items one is willing to collect is only limited to the amount one wants to pay for the pieces. Take fans of the Moody Blues. One of the most collectible items is from 1978's release of *Octave*. London Records issued a neon light, worth about $200. Another "bright" promotional item came courtesy of Jet Records to promote Electric Light Orchestra. The company released both a night-light and an inflatable light bulb to promote the group. Both had the ELO logo stamped on them are worth about $30 a piece.

Elvis Costello fans say one of the most collectible promos is from the 1977 release of *My Aim Is True*. Columbia sent out dart boards to disc jockeys and record store managers. The catch is to find the product still sealed in its original wrappings. If you are lucky enough to find one, hang onto it ... it's worth about $20.

Led Zeppelin collectors say, hands down, the most collectible promotional item from that band is "the object" released in 1976 for the album *Presence.* The black, 12" tall statue is featured on the group's album cover (and throughout the gatefold). The items sells for about $300. But there is a catch in collecting this piece. Forgeries *do* exist. "The easiest way to figure out if you have a real piece or not is to look at the coating of the statue," said Led Zeppelin collector Rick Barrett of Houston, Texas. Barrett says a *real* "object" is made with flat black paint, while a phony piece is made with shiny black paint.

With all of this promotional memorabilia knowledge, your next question is probably, "where can I find all of this stuff?" Good question. First off, if you frequent record shows or advertising pages of *Goldmine,* you'll probably notice dealers asking incredibly high prices for their goods. Now, keep in mind, some of this stuff is, indeed, rare. With only a few thousand pieces ever made in the first place, memorabilia is in a small category of availability. So, a word to the wise, don't be too surprised if you find your once-in-a-lifetime item going for a king's ransom and dealers easily getting the price they want for it.

Another option is to become friendly with your neighborhood disc jockey. These guys (and gals) get packages from record companies on a daily basis. Most of the stuff they'll keep or give to other employees. Other items, they'll trash. (Now, I'm not condoning scavenging through dumpsters at this point.) Call your favorite radio station and ask. The worst they can say is "no." (A piece of advice: Small-market radio stations are usually the best bet for this tactic. Larger markets tend to have countless secretaries and other personnel handle mail and correspondence of upper-level management, such as music or program directors. And, you are more than likely going to receive a "that's not our policy" answer if you ask ... but, hey, go for it.)

No matter what group or singer you collect, chances are you will also find a unique piece of promotional memorabilia to go with them. Both dealers and collectors say the most obscure, the better. So whether you run across a deck of Queen playing cards or a Traveling Wilburys canvas bag, you have also probably run across a unique—and more importantly—collectible, piece to add to your collection.

Press Kits

by Lisa L. Barker

Let's say you finally snagged a copy of your favorite singer's long-out-of-print first album, complete with the bigger-than-life "promo-only" stamp across the backside. What you may, or may not be aware of is that probably wasn't the only item the disc jockey, who originally possessed the disc, had in the package from the record company. Chances are the album might also have contained a press kit, describing the album, its contents, maybe a photo or two of the group/singer and the general biography information that every die-hard fan should already know.

Press kits have always been another angle of collecting any artist, especially for those who have completed their recording collections and are looking for a different collecting avenue. "I consider them the icing on the cake for me," said Sarah Thoms of Davenport, Iowa, who collects Dolly Parton. "I just paid $30 for a *Straight Talk* kit and it only had one picture in it."

"Press kit sales are growing, because of the disappearance of artwork on recordings," said Chris Vincent of Relative Action in Manville, New Jersey. "People want something more tangible with their collections ... an extension if you will."

Vincent has been in the press kit business for about six years, and said older artists still command the big money. "The first Blood, Sweat and Tears press kit is still worth about $100," he said. The kit, for the *Child Is Father To The Man* release in 1968 came in a die-cut folder with sleeves and "tears," along with a vinyl single. Other vintage 1960s kits with high dollar price tags include the first Jimi Hendrix kit, which Vincent said can go for "about $500," and the debut Moby Grape kit, complete with purple suede cover.

Over the past few years, record companies have tended to go overboard on their press releases. The idea was to catch the disc jockey's or record store manager's eye with elaborate, often expensively produced packages. One good case in point is the 1988 press kit release for Jimmy Page's *Outrider* album. The press kit came with a multi-format box, complete with a video interview, cassette and compact disc. The kit came delivered in a lunch box-looking case. "It's worth about $150," Vincent. said

David Bowie fans were impressed with Ryko Records' contribution to the press kit hobby. When *The Rise and Fall of Ziggy Stardust* was re-released in 1990 (Rykodisc LSD-4702), Rykodisc came out with a press kit which contained a vinyl album and a compact disc of the release. The press kit also contained a bio on Bowie and glossies. The kit, if complete and in mint condition can go for up to $150.

But when it comes to who goes for a pretty penny nowadays, Vincent says it's a woman's world. "Debbie Gibson still has a huge hardcore following," he said. "Her *Electric Youth* press kit in its original folder and envelope goes for $50." He said Tori Amos is another artist who might not be enjoying life on the Top 40 charts, but is still number one in the hearts of collectors. "Her *Y Kant Tori Read* kit with the photo and bio can sell for about $125."

But original custom folder press kits are headed for the same graveyard as vinyl. A few years ago, the group Information Society came out with a floppy disc press kit. Although the concept is considered unique and the kit is rare, it is seen as a curiosity piece more than anything and sells for about $25. Another unique piece was from the first Lollapalooza tour. The press release came wrapped around a lollypop, is considered very rare, and sells for about $40. "Those are tough to find," said Vincent. "It's hard to find one with the candy still in one piece."

One common avenue record companies are taking is releasing their press kits in a common folder with the record company's logo on it or a plain, clear plastic, sealed envelope. The kits may or may not contain one or two glossy photos, but most contain a press release on the group's newest recording. The kits do not command the kind of money custom kits do, but average, depending on the group and release, at around $10-20 a piece.

The rage in kits these days appears to be video. VHS tape press kits have been popping up in the pages of *Goldmine* with frequency and seem to be the newest in high dollar items. Groups including Mother Love Bone and R.E.M. have jumped on the video bandwagon, with R.E.M.'s *Automatic For The People* running about $40 with collectors. One video press kit selling well includes Annie Lennox's latest release for *Diva.* The kit came complete with a "video postcard" and a multi-colored box and sells for about $25. "The Coverdale-Page debut is on VHS," Vincent said. "I'm selling it for $50."

The scarcity of press kits is another reason why retailers can get away with selling them with a steep price tag attached. On an average, only a few thousand kits, if that, are printed, placing them in the same rare category as promotional items. The people the kits were meant for – disc jockeys, record store manages, etc. – usually tossed the kits soon after reading them, if they read them at all, dwindling the numbers even further.

"It's a segment of the hobby that's gaining respectability," Vincent said. "The items are special and very unique."

SHOWCASE

Davy's Daydream Believers

*** Member of National Association of Fan Clubs and Authorized by Mrs. Anita Jones ***

Membership Dues: $12.00 Per Year/$15.00 Per Year Overseas

At last, a club on behalf of David Jones in which you can become actively involved! Upon joining, you'll receive a membership kit containing the following:

1) 5x7 Color Photo of David
2) Color Photo Button or Mini Photo Frame
3) Pencil with Club Name Inscribed
4) Photo Pocket Calendar Card or Color Photo Postcard

Newsletters are also a part of your membership package. These will contain updates and full reports on David's activities as well as other Monkees happenings when available. There are special articles in each issue, new photos of David and the Monkees from my own personal collection and discounts on club merchandise offered first to members.

Unique to Davy's Daydream Believers are our own special club projects giving each joining member a chance to be creative and to actually become involved in the whole club experience. Our newsletters alone are quite spectacular, ranging anywhere from 35 pages to 106 pages! Past issues have been dedicated to David's "Oliver" performances in Kansas City in 1988 and the Monkees' British Tour of 1989!

So, come on, join the fun and become part of "Davy's Daydream Believers"!!!

Send your Check or Money Order Payable to:

"DAVY'S DAYDREAM BELIEVERS"
c/o: Debie Sunseri
206 Maple Ridge Drive, Metairie, Louisiana 70001

Purple Flower Gang: Attn: Cindy Bryant, 1803 Lucas St., Muscatine, Iowa 52761. Phone: (319) 263-3607. Beginning its fifth year, this club is recognized by the Monkees and their management and has average involvement with the artists. Special features of the fan club include a fanzine with stories, news, song lyrics, contests, ads, pen pals, reviews, photos, transcripts of radio interviews and the fanzine's own interviews. Cost is $8 (U.S.).

JOHNNY WINTER INTERNATIONAL FAN CLUB

publishes a quarterly newsletter with tour dates, recording plans, interviews, and a trades and exchange column.

Send $10.00 in U.S. or $15.00 International (U.S. Funds) for 1 Year Subscription

To:

JOHNNY WINTER INTERNATIONAL FAN CLUB
2442 NW Market St., #208, Seattle, WA 98107 USA

Tee Shirts and Photo available!

Get B.A.C.K.
(Beatles Appreciation Club of Kansas): Attn: Tony Wedeking, Editor/Publisher, 814 Lindenwood Ave., Topeka, Kansas 66606-1619. Phone 913-233-5205. This fanzine presents a comfortable blend of historic news and views to current articles. Since the Beatles are its business, members are often treated to stories that are rare and unique. Cost $10 U.S., $18 foreign, for membership package and four issues.

Railroad Records

For the eclectic music lover; **Railroad Records** emphasizes diversity with such talent as **HR** (Human Rights), **GG Allin**, **Month Of Sundays** (college/pop), **Drop Circus** (rock) and **Liers In Wait** (gothic/trance). We have t-shirts and posters too! Call or write for a free mail-order catalog: Railroad Records, PO Box 54325, Atlanta, GA 30308-0325 (404) 522-3725, FAX (404) 525-7182.

"MY FAVORITES"

Memorabilia Mail Order Company

"Your Direct Source To The Finest In Music & Celebrity Treasures"

★ Beatles ★ Elvis ★ Stones ★ Madonna ★ Prince ★ Michael Jackson ★ U2 ★ Zeppelin ★ Who ★ BC Rollers ★ Monkees ★ AC/DC ★ Motown ★ 60s

"You name 'Your Favorites' and 'My Favorites' will deliver!"

Vinyl ★ CDs ★ Classic Magazines ★ Gold Albums ★ Autographs ★ Collectibles

Send $1 for postage for FREE CATALOG & STICKER to:

MY FAVORITES
2961 Industrial Rd. #161
Las Vegas, NV 89107

(Include your list of favorite artists/celebrities & want list)
Foreign send U.S. dollar & reply coupon)
24 hr. message line (702) 387-2335 Fax (213) 962-0352

Proper Storage of Recordings

by Stephen Thompson

It isn't hard to work out an efficient system for storing your music collection when you've only got a few dozen LPs and cassettes, and maybe a smattering of compact discs. But for most people, it's difficult to stop there, and most collections eventually become storage nightmares.

What happens when things get out of hand? Most of us have orange crates for LPs and some sort of bookshelf or rack system for cassettes and CDs. But when your ever-increasing CD collection begins to overflow your bookshelf and starts accumulating in boxes—or worse yet, sits in makeshift piles waiting to be knocked over and smashed—you'd better start looking for efficient alternatives.

Fortunately, there are a wide variety of storage systems on the market to alleviate this problem, and more come out all the time. Prices vary widely depending on extravagance, efficiency and volume of storage, but what's important is that there are options.

Arguably the most important feature of any music storage system is that it preserves the quality of the recordings in the best way possible. Most systems cover this criterion adequately, but certain guidelines should always be followed no matter what you do. Heat and humidity have an enormously detrimental impact on the longevity of recordings, including the supposedly immortal compact disc. Humidity warps and waterlogs the paper packaging of LPs as well as the ecopaks/digipaks that house many new CDs, and the damage is permanent. Heat, depending on its intensity, can destroy any recording, whether it be on tape, vinyl or aluminum.

Storage in a cool, dry place is, therefore, a must. Dehumidifiers, though costly, are a worthwhile investment for collectors, but if you can't afford one you should look into picking up a few buckets of calcium chloride compound at your local sporting goods or department store. (These absorb moisture from the air and are usually used to dehumidify boats, tents and the like.) Buckets of calcium chloride are usually small enough to be inconspicuously placed in or around your storage unit.

It's also vital that recordings be kept clear of dust, cigarette smoke and other debris that can harm both the music reproduction and the player itself. Record player needles, tape heads and compact disc player lasers can be ruined over time by dust deposits. Keeping LPs, tapes and discs in their cases when not in use will prevent much of this problem, as will keeping the environment dry and smoke-free. An airtight storage system is ideal for this purpose.

Another way to keep recordings dust and humidity free—particularly LPs and CDs packed in cardboard—is to store them in specially designed plastic bags (preferably ones made of Mylar). Keep in mind that some bags are better than others, and that some really lousy bags can actually release acids over time that damage paper packaging. Shop around and price the competition, but remember that these are essential for the ultimate preservation of LPs. (They've also been known to avert disaster in otherwise nightmarish situations of basement flooding.)

Each recording format (LP, cassette, CD) can be stored in a variety of ways, ranging from cardboard boxes to complex, expensive systems involving drawers, racks and assorted gadgetry. But there are specific criteria to look for with each format.

Vinyl

Vinyl has been around for a long time, and despite what the major record companies tell you, it will never go away entirely. Vinyl's extensive history has allowed for a great deal of experimentation with storage, and most of us came up with our ideal systems years ago. (With the exception of rap and techno DJs, not many people have rapidly growing vinyl collections these days.)

There are systems for storing LPs that work better than the popular orange crates and specially-designed cardboard boxes. Jerry Madziarczyk, who operates the specialty shop CD Storehouse, sells a variety of systems for storing vinyl, including stackable dowel racks. "They stack about four high and hold 100 discs apiece," Madziarczyk said. "They're allegedly made for laser discs, but I've yet to meet anyone who's got 100 laser discs."

The cost? About $50 each.

Madziarczyk himself swears by a simpler, cheaper system. "What I did was buy a metal cabinet like the kind you get at office supply stores," he said. "It's a sealed unit, which you can open and close and, of course, lock. They're a little too deep, but you can adjust the shelves to fit just right."

This system is also preferable because it keeps records away from the elements, and it allows for the placement of a bucket of calcium chloride inside the unit.

Again, be careful to keep your LPs in bags, and take the shrinkwrap off. Shrinkwrap doesn't stop shrinking, and it usually ends up warping and bending the LP sleeve—eventually even the disc itself.

For those LPs that deserve special display, framing may even be in order. To display particularly attractive LP cover art or especially rare pieces, frames can be ideal: They keep out dust and debris, they hold the record flat, and they keep admirers from getting their grubby fingerprints all over everything.

But what if you want an LP framed but you also want to, you know, play it? Frames have a way of permanently imprisoning what they hold, and it kind of defeats the purpose of recorded music to never play what you own. Display cases are another option. Again, these keep onlookers from damaging your most precious items while making it easy to control the climate and access your collection. They also cost a lot of money, take up a grotesque amount of space and make you look snooty. (You might as well string velvet ropes around your collection while you're at it.)

Perhaps the most efficient way to store and display an individual rare/beautiful LP is with a new invention called Swingframe that allows you to open your frame while it's on the wall. Literally two frames in one, Swingframe keeps the LP pressed between two individual frames, which are separated from each other by swinging the top frame open like a door. The hinges holding the frames together are invisible, so it's difficult to tell the difference between this system and an ordinary frame.

Added features of the patent-pending system include custom matting, as well as glass that's specially designed to deflect most ultraviolet rays. Frames can be bought ready-made from the manufacturer, and they come in sizes to fit LPs, comic books, magazines and a variety of other collectibles. For more information and price estimates (they cost in the neighborhood of $40), write Swingframe at the address listed at the end of this article.

Cassettes

Cassettes generally aren't considered collector's items, since the sound quality lacks both the richness of vinyl and the clarity of CD. But cassette sound quality has improved in recent years, and they're far less expensive to acquire than exorbitantly priced CDs. In addition, cassettes' portability makes them extremely convenient, and that factor alone has led to some enormous cassette collections. (Besides, any collector who reviews music on a regular basis has undoubtedly found that cassettes pile up no matter how hard you try to discourage their presence.)

There are various rack systems on the market for cassettes, most of which are variations on CD storage systems (which are described in greater detail in the next section). Like CDs, you'll want a system that keeps cassettes visible from the side; therefore, a shallow storage unit is always best. For smaller collections, little handheld suitcases holding 24 or so cassettes are sold everywhere, and these work great in terms of portability despite the limitations in size.

Madziarczyk—who has access to every rack system imaginable—uses old Xerox paper box lids, which cost nothing and might as well have been made to hold cassettes. And, of course, they're totally stackable.

Compact Discs

Here's where matters get complicated and often incredibly expensive. The storage market is littered with racks made to hold, say, 24 or 36 discs. But the serious music collector would need to buy dozens of these things to hold an entire collection.

However, if you're looking to house a small number of CDs, there are some terrific options. As with cassettes, there are bags/mini-suitcases on the market that allow for portable storage. These usually exist in the form of vinyl gym bags that zip up, and these also work great for keeping CDs dust-free (though you should be careful where you take them).

Flipfiles are another common low-cost, low-quantity storage device. These usually hold about 20 discs in such a way that you can flip through with your finger and view each disc cover. These are cheap, but again, they don't work well in large quantities. If you use them individually, you'll need to store them in such a way that you get a top view. There are cabinets designed to store flipfiles: These allow you to roll out files one at a time and flip through them, but they're a bit costly and complicated for the purpose they serve.

One of the most popular methods of storing relatively small quantities of CDs is vertical racks, which hold about 60 or 70 discs and stand about five feet high. While these generally aren't all that practical (much of your space is taken up by the dividers between CDs), they look sharp in your home or apartment. Made of plastic or metal, vertical racks can usually be connected to one another, making for a larger, somewhat more efficient unit.

There are also binders for CDs that work much the way photo albums do. Unboxed discs are held in plastic pages (four to a page), and space is provided for the storage of disc art. These are popular, but they have their drawbacks: Each book only holds about 40 discs, and you have to fold the ends of the back cover art to fit in the slots.

Compact disc collecting is as addictive a hobby as LP collecting used to be, but CD collections tend to grow noticeably out-of-hand faster because of CDs' width. Therefore, it's not only important to buy a system that holds your existing collection, but you should also be able to account for massive future growth. The more malleable your system is, the happier you'll be in the long run.

Numerous systems are designed to store huge quantities of CDs, though few hold more than 500 pieces. One of the most economical, according to Madziarczyk, is a set of sturdy cardboard boxes with clear plastic lids and slots for individual CDs. Each box costs about $10 and holds 72 CDs, and the boxes are stackable.

Other units are available to hold large quantities of CDs, the most popular being dowel racks and CD bookshelves. Dowel racks are lighter and more economical than the shelves, but Madziarczyk said consumers should take some precautions.

"I would always recommend that if you're going to get a dowel rack you should get one pre-assembled," he said. "There are some sleazy ones out there that say they're easy to assemble, but they wobble a whole lot. I would stay away from anything that doesn't come factory assembled."

But otherwise, dowel racks are a pretty safe bet. Since most of them are carefully treated, the dowels are not known to warp or bow under the weight of a bunch of CDs.

Specially designed bookshelves can be a bit more expensive—they're fairly new on the market and building them requires more materials—but their popularity is growing rapidly. The largest shelving units hold about 500 discs, and the better models, according to Madziarczyk, are Hy-Q (about $130) and Tree Dimensions ($200).

If you're looking to go all out with your shelving, you might want to pick up a bookshelf with glass doors on the front. Expect to pay an extra $50 and sacrifice some storage space (they usually hold about 300 discs), but they look terrific and provide a clean, well-protected, dust-free environment.

One of the most extravagant—and consequently, most expensive—systems is a set of three drawers that holds about 250 to 300 CDs and costs about $250 to $300. You pay for discreet, organized storage, and with extra cost for complicated drawer mechanisms and fancy wood finishes. These often come with extra shelves for your stereo, making up a single convenient music unit.

Cabinet-style systems like those used in some used CD stores are available for about $350. Though not the most attractive or convenient option, these three-drawer units can hold up to 900 discs. (When you've got this many CDs, you might want to look into computer software inventory systems, most of which can be used on IBM.)

Finally, Madziarczyk warns of dealers who will try to sell boxes not intended for CD storage. If dimensions of shelving aren't perfect, jewel boxes can get scuffed up—and while this certainly isn't the end of the world (scuffed up jewel boxes are easily replaced), there's no reason to let it happen.

There are excellent options available to collectors who'd prefer to scrap jewel boxes altogether. A variety of CD sleeves, varying wildly in desirability, is available for slim, efficient storage. But you should be careful when shopping for these.

Paper and cardboard sleeves, though inexpensive, are generally not a good way to store discs, as the material surrounding the disc is too rough. Cardboard in particular also causes problems because the sleeves tend to fit too loosely, allowing discs to fall out and face scuffs and other damage.

Rip-proof paper sleeves (which are made of a tough plastic/paper fiber) are better because they don't cause as many scuffs, but discs fall out of these far too easily.

Probably the best available sleeve is a plastic holder molded around a piece of lint-free cloth. These are sealed on three sides, with a plastic flap that folds over the fourth side to keep the disc from falling out. CD art can be stored behind the cloth, but like CD binders, the back cover art needs to be folded to fit.

But these sleeves offer an added benefit thanks to the porous cloth held between the plastic sheets. Not only is this cloth designed to not produce lint, but it also absorbs dust and dirt that could otherwise stay on the disc and transfer onto the CD player's tracking device.

These sleeves are cheaper and lighter than jewel boxes, and they take up about a third as much space, but you sacrifice your convenient side view when you use this system. ("You have to hold them and thumb through them like a deck of cards," Madziarczyk said.)

You also sacrifice consistency, since many CDs on the market are now being packaged in jewel box-free cardboard containers. You certainly don't want to throw away these boxes; in fact, you should be careful to keep these in plastic bags to prevent scuffing. Despite the aesthetic problems sleeves cause, they allow you to hold a huge amount of discs in something as simple as a shoebox, and that's an unfathomably desirable feature.

Sleeve users can also perform the cunning trick of purchasing 5¼" floppy disc boxes from computer stores or office supply outlets. Sleeved discs fit in these beautifully, and the boxes are dirt cheap.

With all the options available to you, there's no excuse to leave discs, LPs or cassettes lying around unshelved. Recorded music has a finite lifespan: You might as well extend that period by taking some easy precautions. Who knows? With the right shelving system, you could someday make room in your apartment for that bed you've always wanted!

For more information contact:

CD Storehouse, P.O. Box 973, Wilmette, IL 60091

Swingframe, Inc., 10 Buckminster Road, Rockville Centre, NY 11570

Collecting Display Units

by Lisa L. Barker

What would the cardboard industry be without music advertising displays? It seems every time you go into a record store they're everywhere. Those eye-catching mobiles and life-sized stand-ups are all around you for a reason—to remind you to buy that artist's latest offering, just in case you forget. While some of us might give a second glance to a Stevie Ray Vaughn guitar-shaped hanging mobile, others can literally stare for hours, dumb-struck and slack-jawed, at a soaking-wet Vanessa Williams starchly plastered on a three-foot tall stand-up. And still, while some pass them off as another attempt to prompt a buying frenzy for that particular artist's catalog, more often than not, most of those viewing a display really don't pay much attention to them ... unless you collect them.

"Some people buy them to use as shrines for their favorite singers," said Rich Richards of San Diego, California. Richards has been dealing in promotional displays for several years and says he has seen every imaginable trend you can think of with the hobby. "A good example is Duran Duran," he said. "A few years ago I couldn't give them away. With the new album, I've sold a ton of their stuff."

But don't think Richards' clientele is a bunch of frat brothers looking for something to clutter up a dull dorm room. "I have collectors 40 and 50 years old looking to get everything Neil Diamond's or Barbra Streisand's face is on." He said, however, that collectors' tastes vary from region to region. "In the Midwest and on the East Coast, classic rock is hot, but on the West Coast, alternative music displays are swelling."

According to Richards, record companies really got into the "art" of displays in the early 1970s. Groups, including Led Zeppelin, the Moody Blues and Electric Light Orchestra were known, for using inflatable promotion materials, all of which are some of the most sought-after. "The early Led Zeppelin vinyl blimps are still the best sellers," Richards said, adding that they still can command a $300-$500 price. And if something works, well, why not use it again. When the 1990 Led Zeppelin boxed set hit stores, so did its, you guessed it, vinyl blimps. "Those sell for about $150," he said.

Most record companies gave up on display items in the late 1970s when sales began to sag, but some, such as Casablanca, continued promoting its groups with zeal. "The KISS items never lost their appeal," Richards said. "They are the most sought after of all, especially the gigantic one displaying full make-up ... those can still sell for about $500." Even the group's hanging mobiles, in full make-up, of course, garner between $100 and $200 in mint condition.

With the beginning of a new decade and with the help of even flashier entertainers, display advertising made a "come back" of sorts in the 1980s. "You had people like Madonna and Prince that seemed bigger than life that did and still do well on cardboard stand-ups," Richards said. And no matter how "big" the artist is, the "smaller" display will still be a huge collectible. Take, for example, a relatively small five-inch shot of Prince on a motorcycle, promoting the movie (and album) *Purple Rain*. Collectors don't think twice about buying the piece for $50. The same is true for fans of the Material Girl. But ironically, two of Richards' biggest sellers have nothing to do with her latest musical releases. A five inch shot of her in a tight black body suit, fish-net hose, back to the camera and obligatory hand-on-rear promoting the *Unauthorized* biography fetches about $75. "The display she had for her book *Sex* goes for about $150."

What makes displays so collectible are a number of things. Shelf life for one. "The average display only stays up in a store about three to five months," Richards said. "And there are very few that are ever made, which makes them even more collectible." Another reason might be that record companies have caught on to the collectibility of the freebies and have begun to demand that the products be sent back when the stores are through promoting the releases. "I know people in the industry," said Richards. "I also work with trades ... that's how I'm able to get what I have."

And as America gets older, so too, older, more established groups are becoming more popular and in demand, collector-wise. But Richards admitted, reluctantly, that even in death, a popular artist never loses his or her collectibility ... and record companies know this. Take for example recent releases of groups and acts such as Jimi Hendrix, Stevie Ray Vaughn and Freddie Mercury. "It's a shame that when someone dies, their collectibility goes up," Richards said. A three inch tall display of Freddie Mercury, for example, promoting his "latest" album sells for $50. The bland display is just that, compared to the Hollywood Records offering of the brilliant Grandville art for the *Innuendo* album.

Display collectors recommend that after you have located the piece you want to purchase, you try to buy it in the original box for preservation. Most displays are oddly shaped and finding unique-sized boxes after one has bought an item is almost impossible. This is especially true for those who collect "holder" displays.

Record companies can't necessarily trust an 18-year-old record store clerk to properly display their artist's latest musical effort, so companies make it easier by designing nicely packaged displays to hold compact discs and cassettes. These items are equally, if not more so, collectible than regular poster-like displays and standups—but there is a catch—finding holders which aren't yet built. Collectors say holders in the original "virgin" state, complete and unbuilt in their original shipped boxes are worth more than those abused by a possibly careless builder in a frantic hurry to snip, cut and paste.

But more times than not, contrary to what any dealer or collector will advise you to do with your display, display collectors buy displays, in whatever form, to, well ... display.

Sheet Music

by Lisa L. Barker

I've always loved the piano. Sitting in front of the key, humming to myself with nary a care in the world ... except I can't play the piano. I couldn't read the music to save my life. For some unknown reason, I still like to "read" the sheet music though. Learning the words *exactly*, so I won't suffer from the common occurrence of lyricitis and ramble some unintelligible sentence to compensate for my not knowing what the singer is really singing.

"I would guess 90% of the people who buy sheet music can't read music," said Allen Radwill, of Southampton, New Jersey. "They like the pictures or want the words to the songs."

Radwill has been dealing in collectible sheet music since 1980. He said collectors fall into several categories, but most collect the paper goods to see the picture of their favorite performers. "Maybe their favorite singers never put out an album or maybe had one or two singles and the fan doesn't know what they look like, it's a way to visualize them," he said.

In an average Radwill sheet music advertisement, pieces have minimum bids of $8, but he said he has sold other sheets for much more. "I don't want to tell you how much I sold one for, but I think it was sheet music from the Crickets."

He has his own definition of what is highly collectible and what is not. "Here it is in a nutshell," he said. "Pretend it's 1959 and your daughter likes an artist. If you let her go out with him, he's not collectible ... if you don't let her go out with him, he's highly sought after."

Other sheet music collectors agree, the most collectible artists are those who are history ... literally. "Historic pieces do very well with me," said Paul Riseman of Springfield, Illinois. "The most I ever sold a piece for was about $600 for an Irving Berlin sheet of 'Marie,'" he said. "It came out in 1907 and was the first published piece he ever did." Riseman said he found the collectible browsing at an antique sale in a shopping mall. "It would go for much higher now," he added.

But not all historic-era pieces command high price tags. "Stephen Foster is a good example," Riseman said. "Anything found in bound volumes are also hard to sell."

And while most would find offense by the racist connotation, anything with a late 19th to early 20th century African-American on the cover has found a niche. "I won't sell Jim Crow pieces," Radwill. said, "but I've seen pieces go for very high prices." Riseman agrees. "The ragtime sheets are very popular ... anything with blacks on the covers," he said.

Collectors also have found fond favor for movie and Broadway sheets. "Judy Garland, Shirley Temple and the Marx Brothers are big," Radwill said. On that "note," sheet music collectors say, for the true collector, British sheets are the only way to go. "A lot of times, English sheets used totally different pictures than American releases," Riseman said. "There are several sheets I can think of where the song itself was only

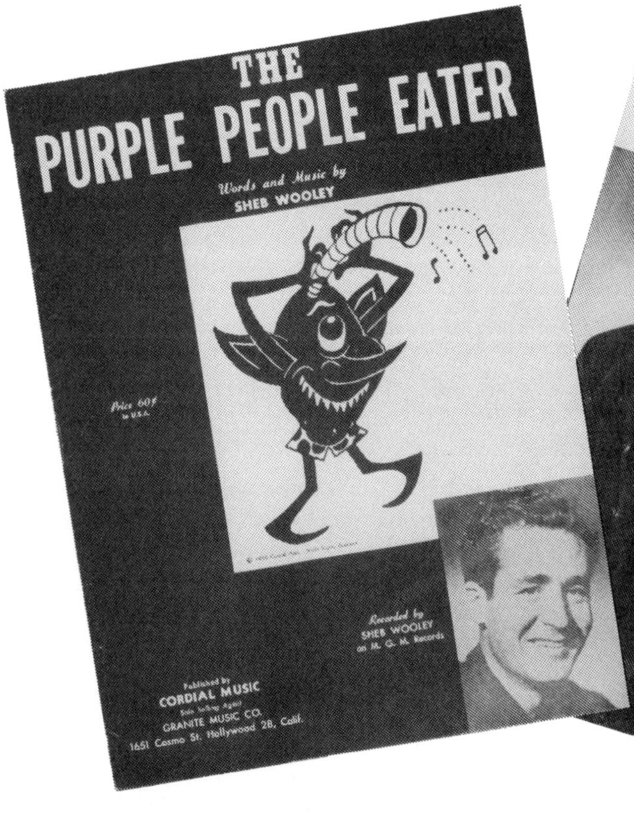

released in the United Kingdom and not in the United States. Those are worth finding." Riseman cited the song "I'm Writing A Letter To Daddy," from the movie *What Ever Happened To Baby Jane* as an example. The music was never released in the U.S. "The same is true for *The African Queen*."

But pinning anyone down on how much collectible sheet music is worth is almost impossible. "I have thousands of pieces of movie sheets that I sell for anywhere from 50¢ to hundreds of dollars," Radwill said. He added that several pieces, including selections from the television shows *Happy Days, Bonanza* and *The Untouchables* sell for about $10-15 a piece.

"It's strange," Riseman said. "On the east coast, for some unknown reason, 'As Time Goes By' (from the movie *Casablanca*) is selling for up to $100 ... but it's only worth about $20-30."

The Theory is, according to Radwill, that whatever is hot on vinyl is hot on sheet music. That statement appears to hold water for him. Radwill said he sells a lot of sheet music from Top 40 artists in both rock and country genres. "Hank Williams and Marty Robbins are doing well ... but so is KISS, the Jackson Five and the Supremes," he said.

But the diversity of the hobby is definitely shown in the diversity of musical tastes. "I have collectors looking for anything by the 13th Floor Elevators to Joni James," Radwill said.

As for newer groups, both the band members and the fans are getting younger and are enjoying the hobby. "Nirvana is hot," Radwill said. However, it seems that *too* young, is bad. "Children's sheet music or teaching books don't sell," Riseman said, "but songs about presidents are very much sought after."

Dealers said they frequent garage sales and flea markets in search for the perfect find. Unlike collecting vinyl, counterfeit music sheets are easy to spot. "All you need to do is look for age," said Hal Phillips, an avid sheet music collector from Philadelphia. "I mean, let's be honest, I'm more likely to buy a piece that's yellowed and shows some wear as opposed to a nice clean white piece."

After you decide which artist you plan to collect, storing sheet music can be tricky. Collectors swear by plastic bags for their investments. "Keep the sheets as clean as you can," Riseman said. "Try not to get anything on them and try to buy them mint, without any wear and tear. Obviously, if you want to sell them later, they have to be in pristine shape."

Or maybe you'll hang on to them and learn how to play the piano after all.

A History of Rhino Records

by Stephen Thompson

Today, Rhino Records has a reputation as the top archival record label in existence, an independent company with more than 1,000 catalog titles and more clout than many major labels. Known for its keen eye for trends and smart sense of humor, Rhino has become a model for other fledgling labels to follow. But the label's origin was a surprisingly inauspicious one.

Rhino began in October 1973, created by Richard Foos as a tiny used record store in Santa Monica, California. (Foos, 44, now serves as president of Rhino Entertainment.) After establishing a partnership with local musician and friend Harold Bronson, now 43, Foos released his first recording in April 1975 – a 7" single titled "Go To Rhino Records," which was sung by local street singer Wild Man Fischer. Every copy of the store's new theme song was given away as an in-store promotion.

Several years of obscurity followed, until Rhino scored its first hit, if you want to call it that: a bizarre 1978 novelty recording of Led Zeppelin's "Whole Lotta Love." Featuring Foos, Bronson and a number of other local musicians, the song was played entirely on an orchestra of kazoos.

Soon after, Rhino released its first full-length album (Fischer's *Wildmania*), which was produced by Bronson for a mere $500. With the local success of *Wildmania*, the Foos/Bronson team – collectively known as the Rhino Brothers – decided to sell their two outlets to business partner Steve Ferber and concentrate more on releasing records.

(There are currently four Rhino stores – two in New York and two in California – and Foos now holds an ownership stake in the chain after buying back the stores in 1989.)

Not long after *Wildmania*, Rhino broke into the reissue market with a picture disc of material by the '60s pop band the Turtles. The label eventually wound up reissuing the entire Turtles catalog as well as (of course) a wide variety of '50s and '60s reissues.

Rhino grew slowly in the next few years, and in 1984 entered the compact disc era with the reissue of the first CDs by the Turtles, Jerry Lee Lewis and the Firesign Theatre. The Firesign Theatre album was the first spoken-word comedy CD in history.

Rhino Home Video made its debut a year later. First on the agenda: *My Breakfast With Blassie*, a parody of *My Dinner With Andre* starring comedian Andy Kaufman and famed pro-wrestler Freddie "Pencil Neck Geek" Blassie. Cult films like *Sleazemania*, *The Lenny Bruce Performance Film* and *Orgy Of The Dead* followed soon after. Today, well over 300 titles occupy Rhino Home Video's catalog, all of which are now distributed through A*Vision, the video arm of Atlantic Records (more on Atlantic later).

Rhino Home Video soon made its mark with previously unreleased '50s and '60s exploitation and horror B-movies. This was made easier by Rhino's licensing agreement with the foreign film company Troma, Inc., which is widely known for such films.

Since its creation, Rhino Home Video went on to release a wide variety of music videos and longform films, and the company wisely tapped into '50s nostalgia by packaging and releasing classic TV shows like *The Lone Ranger*, *Peter Gunn* and *Death Valley Days*.

Rhino's video division currently makes up 10 percent of the company's revenues, but it's been tough for it to compete with the well-financed major film companies. And since most of Rhino's tapes are listed at less than $30, most rental stores don't consider stocking them. (Rental videos usually cost $90 to $100.)

In October 1985, Rhino (the record company) inked a distribution deal with Capitol Records and its parent corporation, CEMA. This pact didn't work as planned – Rhino apparently didn't receive the cooperation it needed from the label – and when the agreement expired Rhino signed a new contract with

the Time-Warner affiliate Atlantic Records.

"I don't know of the specific problems with CEMA, but the deal with Atlantic gives us better opportunities for international distribution," said John Hagelston, manager of national Rhino publicity. "Plus we've got preferred access to the Atlantic catalog, and that's something we didn't have with CEMA, so that was a big plus for us."

In early 1987, Billy Vera & The Beaters gave Rhino another plus: its first #1 Top 40 single with "At This Moment" from the hit TV series *Family Ties*. The single—and the album from whence it came (*By Request: The Best Of Billy Vera & The Beaters*)—both went gold.

That same year, the Monkees' comeback had climaxed, affording huge sales for the band's Rhino reissues. Though the release of *Pool It* (the Monkees post-comeback studio album on Rhino) tanked, the reissues showed evidence of the label's often brilliant timing.

Rhino's growth and progress continued in the next few years, and in January 1990 the label launched the first five of what was originally planned to be 15 (but eventually became 22) volumes of its famed *Have a Nice Day: Super Hits of the '70s* series. As evidenced by the number of volumes, these collections stand among Rhino's most popular releases.

"I think we've done our last volume of that," Hagelston said with a laugh. "We've hit the bottom of the barrel and probably even gone underneath, so as far as I know, Volume 22 is the last."

The same year marked the debut of Rhino's Word Beat spoken word label as well as reissues by Johnny Cash, Willie Nelson, Merle Haggard and Buck Owens—releases that preceded the country music explosion by about a year.

In February 1991, the new Kid Rhino label began reissuing classic Hanna-Barbera recordings and put out new children's music by Bobby Goldsboro and former Monkee Micky Dolenz. Since its inception, Kid Rhino has grown in popularity, tapping into the children's market before Barney the much-despised purple dinosaur began selling millions of records and renewing mainstream interest in children's recordings.

"We don't have any juggernauts like Barney yet, although we're hoping we've got a deal with Steven Spielberg to release recordings tying in with the "Animaniacs" series that he's done," Hagelston said. "We've got really high hopes for that."

Kid Rhino will be issuing some "Three Stooges" and "Flintstones" albums soon, as well as some releases in conjunction with McDonald's restaurants. Another Kid Rhino project causing some excitement is a concept album titled *Primary Colors*, which tells the story of a creature from the rain forest named Meeps, who wanders into the big city and becomes a media celebrity.

Featuring alternative rock celebrities from bands like X, Red Hot Chili Peppers, Beastie Boys, Toad the Wet Sprocket, Mary's Danish, The Posies and School of Fish, *Primary Colors* should come out early in 1994.

Soon after the establishment of Kid Rhino, the semi-annual Rhino Awards made their debut. The first set of Rhinos, awarded to artists responsible for the year's most dubious contributions to popular music, went to Vanilla Ice, Madonna, New Kids On The Block, Warrant, Poison and M.C. Hammer.

In April 1992, Rhino signed its aforementioned distribution deal with Atlantic Records and began the huge—but immensely profitable—task of reissuing classic Atlantic masters from the '50s through the '70s.

Atlantic's fabulous catalog includes numerous studio recordings by Aretha Franklin, Otis Redding, Ray Charles, Wilson Pickett and Sam & Dave, as well as the amazing Stax/Volt singles library. Several hundred titles have been released since the announcement of the Atlantic/Rhino pact, including the definitive nine-volume Stax/Volt boxed-set.

Seven months after signing with Atlantic, *The Righteous Brothers: Anthology (1962-1974)* became the label's second gold album, contributing to yet another record year for Rhino revenue. In 1992, Rhino grossed a total of $55 million despite noto-

Rhino's Grammy-winning *Aretha Franklin: Queen Of Soul* boxed set

riously recessionary times. And though $55 million is a relatively small figure compared to that generated by giants like Columbia or Warner Bros., it's a full $15 million more than Rhino made the previous year.

In February 1993, Rhino followed commercial success with a critical achievement in the form of its long-deserved first Grammy: Best Liner Notes for *Aretha Franklin, Queen of Soul: The Atlantic Recordings*.

A month later, the label took a major risk, announcing the creation of its new FORWARD label and the signing of Todd Rundgren (TR-I), NRBQ and Beausoleil (whose most recent record—released in April—was FORWARD's first release). It's still far too early to gauge the label's success, but Rundgren's *No World Order* came out last July and hasn't exactly broken sales records since.

"Our sales department is actually pretty pleased with the sales figures given that he's not touring at the moment and there isn't a great deal of radio play," Hagelston said, adding that Rhino has always had a difficult time coming up with the money to break into the contemporary music market.

"That's one reason for the direction we've chosen for FORWARD," Hagelston said. "Basically, we're restricting it to artists that have a built-in audience base and a lot of name recognition. This time we're not trying to break people that no one's ever heard of before."

In the past, Rhino made attempts at breaking new talent with the unsuccessful RNA (Rhino New Artists) label, which folded after producing a shortage of bankable hits. According to Hagelston, that label's main problem was the audience it was trying to reach.

"A lot of people that were on RNA had a lot of exposure on the college alternative market, but not an awful lot with a larger mainstream audience," Hagelston said. "We're trying to pick people now with a little bit better identity with your average rock buyer as opposed to your average tight college student."

"We didn't have as good a feel for how to market RNA college artists," he said, "so we figured we'd stick with classic rock, which is—certainly in terms of reissues—our stock in trade."

An even bigger problem for Rhino, and it's one that still haunts most independent labels, has been that artists often bail out on a small label when their albums become even marginal hits.

Both the Beat Farmers and House of Freaks were swiped away from Rhino by larger labels (Curb and Reprise, respectively) when Rhino couldn't afford the overhead to compete with large-scale offers. FORWARD has the benefit of Atlantic distribution, but there still haven't been any major hits.

RNA has been one of only a few unsuccessful Rhino ventures, joining such widely forgotten efforts as the Monkees' *Pool It* and a late-night comedy series ("Club Rhino") for ABC that never even aired. But those missteps aside, Rhino has an extremely impressive track record.

Rhino Home Video's "The Panama Deception" added an Oscar to the label's list of critical achievements, winning the award for Best Documentary in 1993. And just this past June, Rhino co-sponsored the successful Troubadours Of Folk festival at UCLA. The two-day event, dubbed a Lollapalooza for baby boomers, was inspired by Rhino's Troubadours Of The Folk Era, Vols. 1-3 anthologies.

Rhino's staff has a wide variety of new plans for the coming months and years, including still more Rhino/Atlantic reissues. The label recently began releasing definitive reissues of the Atlantic jazz catalog, an interactive CD-ROM based on the *Blues Masters* series is planned for release in 1994.and Rhino expects to break into book publishing, TV and film production soon.

"The book situation is very amorphous," Hagelston said. "I haven't really heard of any specific projects, but we're in the very early planning stages of producing some lower-budget films. We're actively looking into that, but that's further along the line than the books."

As for CD-ROM, Rhino has already entered the market with the Rundgren album, which Hagelston says is the first interactive record release in history. Rundgren conceptualized the music on *No World Order* to be broken into small snippets of sound that can be pieced together in a variety of ways using a special computer program.

"If you listen to the music on the straight CD version, you can hear how he's made the music a lot more modular," Hagelston said. "There are elements of rap and sampling to make it easier to juggle the parts in a certain way."

Such ambition has always played a key role in Rhino's success, but it's hard to overlook the quality of many of the releases themselves. Rhino reissues are almost always lovingly recreated, with meticulous packaging, insightful liner notes and attractive graphics. Tracks are always digitally remastered, usually using original masters, and discs tend to be packed to the maximum. (The norm is 18 to 22 tracks in 70 or so minutes, though Rhino has occasionally been known to skimp on compilations like the recent *Faster & Louder* hardcore punk sets.)

"Our engineer, Bill Inglot, is probably the best in the business," Hagelston said. "In fact, a lot of other companies will turn to him when they've got a reissue they want to put together."

"We've been doing this for 15 years," he continued, "so we've got some pretty good sources of rare photographs and experts within any given genre who can write authoritative liner notes."

No chintzy, bargain-basement mail-order pop compilations. No reliance on ill-conceived "tribute" albums like the ones that clutter the shelves of many independent record stores. And nothing that's been done by other record labels already.

Though its distribution is provided by Atlantic, Hagelston said Rhino benefits largely from its ability to draw material from a variety of labels.

"Probably the most important thing about the Rhino reissues is the extent to which we'll look to cross-license stuff," he said. "A lot of labels just reissue what they've got in their catalog, whereas Rhino will go out knocking on the doors of as many labels as possible, looking for all the artist's biggest hits and most significant recordings."

In addition, like most independent labels, Rhino's retail pricing is almost always well below that of the ludicrously overpriced majors: CDs usually list at $13.98, a full three dollars below the standard cost of major label releases.

Finally, like any successful business, Rhino has demonstrated a savvy for efficiently dealing with mass audiences. Over 120,000 mailing list subscribers receive the bi-monthly Rhino catalog, and the mail order division (which now includes infomercials) supplies a substantial portion of Rhino's business.

On the management front, every Rhino department (total staff: 100) has a say in the development of releases, even when certain employees wouldn't otherwise be viewed as experts. Each staff member benefits from a laid-back management style, which even includes a generous supply of beanbag chairs for quarterly staff meetings.

Consequently, employee morale is reportedly quite high (everyone who provides input on a given project gets credit in liner notes), and the label receives a generous amount of consumer advice and input from within.

Management strategies aside, Rhino's involvement in successful charitable endeavors such as Rock the Vote and the successful Ban the Box campaign have provided the label with good PR both within Rhino and outside of it. On the plate now: plans to donate a percentage of profits to organizations dedicated to AIDS research, environmental organizations, preservation of indigenous cultures, humane societies, Amnesty International and many more. In addition, part of Rhino's new headquarters in Santa Monica—which, incidentally, are twice the size of its old location—now serves as Rock the Vote HQ.

But Rhino has worries ahead. With a shortage of catalogs left to reissue—and with more majors like Columbia deciding to make money from their own reissues—Rhino's large-scale future could be in jeopardy. It's incredibly complicated, difficult and expensive for Rhino to involve itself in the purchase of master recordings. The label simply doesn't have the overhead it needs to purchase permanent rights to catalogs (it can only license them as reissues), and consequently Rhino makes less money in the long run. This accounts for much of why $55 million is good but not spectacular for a label as large and successful as Rhino.

But, not surprisingly, Rhino has aces in the hole. First and perhaps most importantly, no major label is willing to bank on artists whose work isn't widely remembered. But on Rhino's scale, if an album sells 20,000 copies it turns a respectable profit. The big six major labels can't afford to deal in such small figures, so the market for B-list reissues is left open to Rhino and other indies.

"One of the big secrets in terms of how Rhino operates involves keeping costs down, particularly in terms of oddball releases," Hagelston said.

To justify release of an album, Rhino only needs to press 10,000 copies, and it costs as little as $30,000 to put out a given record. By comparison, most majors invest several hundred thousand dollars in a single studio album.

Second, Rhino is and may always be the premier reissue label, with an even wider reputation for quality than other respectable labels like Rykodisc and Razor & Tie. (Rykodisc has, however, had remarkable luck with new artists like the mega-successful, Bob Mould-led alternative rock band Sugar.)

Rhino also possesses a keen eye for knowing when trends are on their way—a quality the label has displayed throughout its existence. Country music. Compact discs. Children's music. '70s nostalgia, and other kitsch. Reissues themselves. Rhino was the first to really tap into a previously unforeseen market for boxed-sets, and it remains the industry's most respected archivist.

Finally, nostalgia is bound to strike every generation. Much to the dismay of Baby Boomers, today's college students already relish "early '80s" hits as beloved golden oldies, and there's no reason Rhino can't tap into that market with a few dozen volumes of, say, *Help Yourself: Super Hits of the '80s*.

Rhino has only begun to explore this avenue with the *DiY* punk volumes and the aforementioned *Faster & Louder* sets. There's no reason to believe Rhino won't soon put out collections featuring the hits of A Flock Of Seagulls, Dexy's Midnight Runners and Big Country. Each could be marketed on college campuses nationwide.

"There's been talk around the office of an '80s series, but I'm not sure exactly what it'll involve yet," Hagelston said. "I do know that there's a set like that in the planning stages."

"There are other labels that are looking into doing something similar," he continued. "We have to make sure our compilations will be the definitive look at the Reagan Years."

Was there ever any doubt?

Harold Bronson and Richard Foos, known as the "Rhino Brothers."

Tour Programs

by Lisa L. Barker

All right, let's see a show of hands. How many of us go to a concert and buy a souvenir T-shirt, only to wear it once, wash it (and shrink it) and throw it in a drawer, never to be seen again, except to wear when everything else is dirty?

We all get duped into buying them and curse ourselves when we spend $30 on a shoddy tee with an iron-on transfer which faded halfway through the rinse cycle. But collectors insist there is another way to remember your once-in-a lifetime concert ... a tour program.

"It's a piece of memorabilia, a way to remember the show visually, when you can't take a camera in." said Jeff Holmboe of Concert Express in Hopkins, Minnesota.

But dealers say their big business comes from those who don't even attend the shows. "Some collect for the investment," Holmboe said. "It's like baseball cards to a fan of a certain artist. They have to have everything that group or person's face is on."

"It's a visual art piece," said dealer/collector Bill Glahn of Bentonville, Arkansas, who added that the most collectible programs are not from the mega-tour 365-days-a-year groups, but from some of the most unlikeliest performers. "I'm always running out of anything from the Bee Gees, Ratt or the Bangles. I can't keep them in stock," he said. Still, there are other groups dealers can't seem to get rid of at almost giveaway prices. "Cinderella, Great White and INXS are impossible to dump," Holmboe said. "'80s groups don't sell well for me," said Glahn. "I can't even sell the Cars or Men At Work stuff for a buck." Glahn said that the once-chart topping Aussie group is known by dealers as a "poison" item. "I won't go near them," he added.

Collectors and dealers alike are unsure which group first got the concert program trend going, but all admit the older the piece, the more likely it is to be a collectible.

"I think the festival shows sell the best," Glahn said. "One of the most expensive pieces I can think of in that category is the 22-page Texas International Pop Festival program in 1969. The psychedelic covered souvenir featured a page of Led Zeppelin and is hard to come by in good shape." Glahn said that piece, if in great shape, will easily sell for about $400. "Another piece that everyone is on the lookout for is the Pocono Music Festival in 1972. It has a feature on Badfinger," he added.

Enthusiasts say benefit concert programs are other highly sought after pieces. A check of *Goldmine* finds that the 1990 Kenworth concert program, for example, still sells for in excess of $100.

But when it comes to consistent collectible tour programs, everyone agrees that rock 'n' roll is here to stay. "Guns 'N Roses and Van Halen are always great sellers," said Glahn. "I had about 1,000 Def Leppard programs from the Hysteria tour ... we sold them in a matter of days for $23 a piece," said Holmboe. "Anything with Led Zeppelin, Black Sabbath or Ozzy Osbourne is huge ... and of course every Rolling Stones program is a must," he added.

In fact, dealers say one of the most expensive items they recollect is a 1971 Japanese Led Zeppelin tour program. "It could easily sell for $500," Glahn said. "It's getting to be where some of these guys aren't going to be around much longer," said Holmboe. "You have to get everything you can while they are around."

As with the 1971 Led Zeppelin tour program, Japanese tour books are sought after but expensive. Artists such as Madonna and Michael Jackson have had huge success overseas on tour, and even more success back home with the interest in their foreign collectibles. "Artists usually only play maybe four or five shows in, lets say, Japan. Those programs are very difficult to come by," Glahn said.

When beginning a collection, all agree that the best place to buy a program is at a venue. "There is a lot of counterfeiting out there," said Glahn. "You have to know what the original looks like to know if you have a phony." If you don't buy a program at a concert, dealers recommend you look carefully at the printing and the color before buying it anywhere else. "If the printing looks blurred or if the colors seem fuzzy, then it's probably a copy," Glahn said.

According to dealers, there are legitimate re-issues of classic tour programs. "A lot of people go that route, because it's easier to buy, let's say, a Beatle's program, for $6, than it is to buy an original one for ten times that amount," Glahn said.

If you are unable to attend a show, dealers say that if the venue is part of a long-running state-by-state tour, your chances

of getting a program are better due to the over-stock of leftover books. Shorter, selective tours tend to offer limited editions of programs, making them hard to come by. "One example I can think of is when the Who toured a few years back for the Tommy anniversary," Glahn said. "I think there were only two shows, one in Los Angeles and one in New York. They gave out these little 20- or 30-page pamphlets. They sell for about $10 now."

Some artists, by reason of feeling giving or guilty over the price of concert memorabilia, offer free programs to those attending shows. At the last two Paul McCartney tours, patrons were offered a gigantic (and some say over-priced) "official" program, with nothing more than airbrushed pictures of the band inside. But, if you were paying attention to the ushers, you were also offered a big, book-sized, better edited, fact-filled and free program to go along with the torn ticket stub. "Some people threw those away," Glahn said. "The collectors still have them ... who knows, in a few years they might be worth something."

Another new way for artists to market their show memorabilia is through video. Recent concert tours from Elton John and others have offered VHS tapes of the artists "preparing" for a tour and even throwing in the latest visual renditions of their new, soon-to-be-released tunes.

Whatever amount of money you put into your collection, collectors recommend that as soon as you buy your item, store it properly in a quality plastic, preferably sealed, bag. "If you are going to re-sell it later on down the road, condition is a prerequisite to a good price," Glahn said. Even small bends or creases in the program can cause the price to literally plummet.

Ain't Nothing But The Reel Thing

by Lisa L. Barker

Does anyone remember when record clubs had a choice of reel-to-reel tapes in their applications for membership? Some collectors wish record companies continued to give music lovers (and collectors) that same option. The long-dead format, which went the same way as the 8-track tape, is still as collectible as ever and some believe they are still some of the best recordings ever made.

"It's just not true that they had an inferior sound quality," said Gary Johnson from Rockaway Records in Los Angeles. "They are awesome quality and audiophiles love them." And apparently collectors still love them. Johnson said reel-to-reel selections from artists such as the Beatles sell out as soon as he gets them in the store.

The manufacturer of reel-to-reel tape recordings ceased in

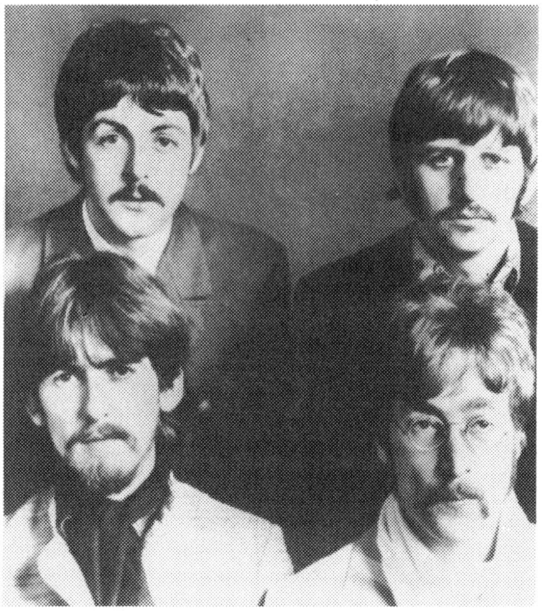

The Beatles

The Rolling Stones

"The only ones that collectors really want are from four artists ... the Beatles, Bob Dylan, the Beach Boys ... and of course, the Stones"

The Beach Boys

Bob Dylan

the late 1970s, when cassettes were taking over and inching out both the 8-track and reel-to-reel. "Actually you can thank the record clubs for keeping them alive for as long as they did," Johnson said. Record clubs such as Columbia continued to offer the recording option long after record stores pulled the sale of the items off the shelves.

But collectors seem to agree that the only true collectible reel-to-reel tapes are from a limited number of artists and groups. "The only ones that collectors really want are from four artists," said Dave Conway, author of the Rolling Stones fanzine *Gimme Shelter.* "the Beatles, Bob Dylan, the Beach Boys ... and of course, the Stones."

Tom Grosh of the record store Very English and Rolling Stone agreed. "Classic rock is the way to go—with the original cover art." Grosh, who is also a Rolling Stones collector from Lancaster, Pennsylvania, said one of the most collectible reel-to-reels is the Rolling Stones' *Their Satanic Majesties Request,* complete with the original 3-D artwork on the cover. Grosh estimates the 1967 release is worth close to $100.

The first reel-to-reel releases came in the early 1960s. The reels were released on two speeds, 3¾ and the more popular, 7½. They were, more or less, just a smaller version of the popular album format, with the front bearing the same artwork as the vinyl and the back side usually featuring song listings, credits and general information on the band. Collectors say the way to tell a true reel-to-reel recording is whether the tapes themselves have labels pasted on them with the title and artist. Beatles collectors say the Fab Four were the first in America to release the format, in 1964, with 5" reels, released in both mono and stereo.

"The Beatles released *Meet The Beatles.* They also released *"Yesterday" ... and Today* in 1966, but only with the trunk cover," Johnson said. "I've sold *Meet The Beatles* in mono for about $200" he added.

The Beatles were also some of the few artists who released double recordings on one tape. In 1965, *Beatles '65* and *Early Beatles* were released on one recording as well as *Beatles VI* and *Something New.* Artists including Jefferson Airplane and Elvis Presley also released duo recordings on one tape during the same time period. Dealers put the value, on at least the Beatles' double recordings, at around $100.

Dealers also admit that, even though reel-to-reel recordings can command a good price, they command a better price if still sealed. "Take for instance *Sgt. Pepper's,"* said Rockaway's Johnson. "It's worth about $40 as is, but sealed, it's liable to get anywhere from $60 to $75." Occasionally, tapes also included liner notes and lyric sheets inside the boxes. "I know both John Lennon's *Imagine* and *Plastic Ono Band* releases contained lyric sheets inside," Johnson said.

But, contrary to what some say, others argue that the Beatles are not the only collectible reel-to-reel group around. Led Zeppelin fans say the five Zep' albums released on the tape format are worth mentioning. Zep collectors say only the group's first four "numbered" albums and *Houses Of The Holy* were the only ones Led Zeppelin ever released on reel-to-reel.

"The first three tapes were released with roman numerals on the spines of the boxes," said Houston Led Zeppelin collector Rick Barrett. "But on *Led Zeppelin IV,* instead of the numerals, they had the four symbols." Barrett said the tapes are worth about $20-$30 a piece.

One reel-to-reel piece Barrett is proud of involves the 1969 release of what is commonly called *Led Zeppelin II.* "I have two different versions of that one," Barrett said, "the regular release, with the roman numerals on the spine, and a second one with the roman numerals and the phrase 'The Only Way To Fly' on it." Barrett said the unusual variation is not a bootleg, but an authentic release from Atlantic Records. "I think it is very rare," he said. "I guess it's worth between $100 to $200." But he insists the find is not for sale at any price.

Some argue when exactly it was that record companies or record clubs stopped making reel-to-reel releases. "I think it was around 1978," Johnson said. "Two I can think of immediately are Elvis Costello's *Armed Forces* and Bruce Springsteen's *Darkness On The Edge Of Town.* Johnson said he believes both releases are worth about $30-$40 a piece.

Collectors say reel-to-reel is a new avenue fans of a certain artist have to keep their collections complete. "You've got the records and the picture sleeves ... so what's next?" Conway said.

The Bowling Green State University Sound Recording Archives:

A Collection Development Case Study

by Professor William L. Schurk

The Audio Center, as Bowling Green State University Library's Sound Recordings Archives was originally named, was conceived on paper in the mid-1960s, when plans for a new campus library were being formulated. When the new main library (William T. Jerome Library) was opened for service in 1967, one half of the third floor had been allocated for the Center to house its beginning recordings collection, support book material, and listening services.

The Library administration's original intent was that the Audio Center would furnish sound recordings and listening facilities to those campus areas that heretofore had not been afforded such services. A language laboratory, the School of Music listening lab, and Instructional Media Center already existed, however students and faculty members who wanted access to recorded plays, poetry and prose reading, folk music, and the like had nowhere to turn. The Audio Center was expected to fill these needs.

The Audio Center opened for service in early 1968 with a shelf full of recordings, newly installed listening equipment and booths, and subscriptions to *Billboard* and *Schwann* magazines. At this same time, popular culture as an academic discipline was being promoted by Dr. Ray Browne, who had recently joined the Bowling Green faculty as a professor in the Department of English. The new program began to mature, soon to develop into an internationally recognized and respected Center for the Study of Popular Culture, a separate Department of Popular Culture, the Popular Press, and the Popular Culture Library. These four areas of study were simultaneously being promoted through the expanded material selection policy within the Audio Center.

Since music plays such a key role in the study of popular culture, restructuring the Center's selection policy to expand it's holdings of commercially released popular recorded material and the acquisition of such material began in earnest. Initially, local radio stations in Bowling Green, Toledo, and Fostoria, Ohio were contracted for regular donations of both duplicate and unneeded recordings. This resource system, even after 25 years, still has proven to be quite fruitful. The Sound Recordings Archives, as the Audio Center is now named, still acquires compact disc albums and singles in this manner, even though the LP and 45 rpm gifts have all but disappeared, expect for an occasional stash of old public service announcements, syndicated music shows, and radio production source material.

In addition to those traditionally recorded genres included in the collection and noted earlier, the Archives' holdings also include all forms of popular music, from rock, soul, reggae, rhythm and blues, new wave, punk, heavy metal, rap, and hip hop, to jazz, blues, gospel, country, rockabilly, zydeco, and Cajun, to sermons, documentaries, big band, and movie and television music. All conventional (and some unconventional) recording sizes and speeds are included, with total piece count of cylinders, discs, and tape reaches over 600,000. The open real tape holdings include over 4,000 hours of old-time radio shows and the BGSU Living Archives. The Living Archives, which began as a series or oral interviews with popular authors, has not been expanded to include interviews with figures in the public eye, air-shots from radio and television, and collected commercial and transcription recordings of early country music performers.

The formidable support print collection consists of thousands of monographic histories and biographies, song books, and reference tools including all major discographies, biographical dictionaries, and trade catalogs. The periodical collection is a particularly valuable component of the Archives because of the need for immediacy for current information from such trade publications as *Billboard, Cashbox, Record World* (now defunct), and *Radio and Records* and the publication of discographical and biographical articles in such journals as *JEMF Quarterly, Record Exchanger Record Research, Journal of Country Music* and the Association for Recorded Sound Collections *Journal.* The magazines also serve as an excellent acquisition source with auction lists and advertisements of peripheral and obscure recordings. Among the 100-plus current subscription titles held are *American Music, Bluegrass*

Unlimited, Contemporary Christian Music, Sixteen, Down Beat, Goldmine, Rolling Stone, and *Stereo Review,* with backfiles of such defunct titles as *Beetle, Zoo World, New Kommotion, Different Drummer, Bam, Bam Boom, Record Changer,* and *Muleskinner News.*

Highest priority for cataloging the recordings has been to enter records into the nationally accessible ODLC library database, located in Dublin, Ohio. That information in then made accessible to the newly installed OhioLink database to which the University employs as its local library indexing system. Here is included not only complete album cataloging information, but also access to all major recording groups and individuals, every song title on each LP, and appropriate subjects. The use of the Archives extends far beyond the local University community. Scholars and students throughout the nation, Western Europe, the Far East, and Australia correspond with and visit the Archives to engage in serious studies. In addition, commercial record companies have on occasion made use of the original and rare recordings for either reissue or reference endeavors. It has worked closely with Time-Life Music, the Smithsonian Institution, Rhino Records, Old Homestead Records, and Rykodisc in these efforts.

Until the late 1960s there was almost no interest or inclination for any American university to actually create a sound recording collection of popular music to support an academic program. True there were scattered courses being taught at institutions of higher learning that had a bent towards teaching lyric content, musical style, or social implication of popular song, but no university had up to that time taken the big step to actually treat popular music as more than a musical and poetic stepchild or phenomenon.

Popularly disseminated music of the first 60 years in America was traditionally represented in college curriculums through the thorough examination of jazz, blues, folk music, and to some extent, musicals. It was unthinkable however for an academic program to support anything musical that had even a smattering of mass dissemination. that meant that rock and roll, rhythm and blues, country and western, and even calypso music were the most forbidden of topics to tackle in university teaching up until at least the late 1960s.

In the first place, up to the mid '60s, no one ever wrote extensively about popular music from the eye of a consuming public. If at all there appeared a treatise on scat singing, the twist, or bluegrass music, it would undoubtedly flow from the pen of an outside observer, one looking within from a more controlled world of more popularly accepted music forms. Only the advent of real "rock journalism" making its first appearance in the mid-1960s in the form of magazines such as *Rolling Stone, Creem*, and *Crawdaddy*, was there a conscious effort to judge popular/rock music on its own musical, artistic, and social merits. Even then the academics were slow on picking up these signals that this most widely persive phenomenon would (and always did) play such an important part of the American youth culture.

If a library, either college or public, would have even a small collection of monographs interpreting the various popular musical styles, a supporting recordings collection would almost never exist along side. Usually there would be a pleasure or recreational listening collection located in a highly accessible area, such as part of a University's larger "serious" recordings collec-

Professor William L. Schurk in the Bowling Green Archives

tion or a public library's "young adult" section.

What was completely ignored was the fact that there was actually a large body of material which could be studied, analyzed, and written about. Meaning that published analyses had to be created from the author actually having to listen to some popular music. If this initial step was not taken the work would be inaccurate, incorrect, uninspired, and completely devoid of any serious merit.

How can one study the lyric content and musical harmonies of Hank Ballard and the Midnighters without listening to their recordings of "Sexy Ways," "60 Minute Man," and "Work With Me, Annie"? The interpretation of Duane Eddy's or Link Wray's guitar styles would be non-existent without one giving a hard listen to their great recordings: "Rebel Rouser" and "Detour" by Eddy and "Rawhide" and "Rumble" by Wray, for example. And if the influence of Caribbean music on American rock were to be approached, recordings of the calypso of Sparrow, the blue beat of Millie Small, and the reggae of Bob Marley cannot be ignored.

The ultimate goal of any academic library that would purport to create and maintain a serious popular music research collection would be to have one central area where books, periodicals, reference tools, and recordings all coexisted in one physical area. Such a collection should not be split between floors or even buildings to accommodate the varying formats. A listening area, the stacks of books and periodicals, and the recordings should all be together in one place.

There can be no better way for this author to speak of the "art" of sound recordings collection development than by presenting his own experiences while creating what is considered to be the largest and most comprehensive popular music research center in an American academic institution.

It should be rightfully assumed and expected that a popular recordings collection which exists in a college or university would have a reason for being. Gone are the days when a college had money to burn and would accumulate such a collection solely for the pleasure and recreation of its student body. An established academic program should already be in place or at least a strong proposal for such a program to exist would be nearing the acceptance stages in order that popular recordings would be seriously considered for inclusion in a library collection. At the least a core of classes should be offered which would require the use of popular recordings, either as part of an inclusive department of popular culture, as selected popular music courses being offered in an array of academic disciplines such as music, theater, sociology, and film studies, or as a support collection for practical production needs for technology and radio/television students.

Major components which make up the activity of popular recordings administration such as cataloging, housing, staffing, security, preservation techniques, and use control, are outside the scope of this article and will not be discussed. All are as equally important as the selection of materials but each deserves its own separate in-depth treatment.

Three major factors that go into building a popular recordings collection include having a workable acquisitions budget,

Displays in the archives showcase regularly showcase various genres, record labels and musical themes (which in the past have included as diverse a topic as "Wrestling records"). The display shown here is dedicated to the Stomp-Off record company

creating a strong collection development policy, and selecting an appropriate complement of sound carriers.

A realistic acquisitions budget must be sought in order that a continuum of purchasing of current product be maintained throughout the school's fiscal year. There is never a week that passes without new recordings being introduced into the market, and just as quickly recordings go out of print. Other than "hit" recordings much recorded material can and does have a short life of existence. Once a recording goes out of print it may never be made available again or at the last return to the collectors' market at a much higher price. Limited pressings of key recordings is a basic fact of the business. Plus, if a library does choose to go the route of the used record trade for older 78s, 45s, and LPs to supplement the new recordings, a ready supply of funding should be available to ensure that an instant purchase of a once-only opportunity is not passed by.

A suggested annual budget amount cannot be made here since each collection will take on a personality and holdings profile of its own, all based on a number of institutional factors such as university budget, space allocated for the collection, and actual academic needs. If new compact discs are the only recordings to be purchased it can be assumed that they can cost anywhere from about eleven to fifteen dollars each, depending on the source for purchases. Used recordings, including 78s, 45s, LPs, and even CDs, can vary in price from 10¢ up to hundreds of dollars each. Judicious and comparative buying can of course assure that the dollar be stretched that much further and more recordings can be purchased.

Equally as important as obtaining a workable budget is the creating of a strong collection development policy. This policy should spell out priorities for inclusion. Traditionally the list would include that which the collection was to serve, the genres (or subjects) of recording material to be collected, and the sound carrier formats that were to be employed.

The sound carrier is most important because this gives provision for the library to decide whether it will only acquire the new compact disc format, or also include LPs, 45s, and 78 rpm discs, audio tape formats such as cassette, open reel, and 8-track, or even wire or cylinder recordings. Understandably most libraries won't even consider the less conventional or older formats such as 8-tracks, wire recordings, and cylinders but much of the other formats are still readily available. In fact, even though CDs are rapidly becoming the sound format of choice, new vinyl LPs are still available in limited quantities, and cassette-only material continues to be made available, but here for mostly alternative productions.

If the choice is made by the library to buy only new compact discs the selection chore is made easier since the prices, as mentioned earlier, will be more standardized, and new selection tools generally refer to only CD release numbers for easy ordering. This also means that the only playback equipment that has to be purchased are compact disc players and probably cassette players for the possibility of playing purchased cassettes and to make taped copies of recorded excerpts for teaching purposes. Compact discs, for all the controversy surrounding their existence, appear now to be accepted by most as the playback medium of the present. I have found that a purchasing arrangement with a local store is the best for buying CDs. The store stock can be browsed on a regular basis, special orders can be placed, and most important of all, if the library becomes a major and steady customer, there should be no question that a discount deal could be struck.

Notwithstanding the almost universally accepted fact that CDs actually sound better than their vinyl counterparts (no pops, clicks, surface noise, or skipping or sticking—usually), there is also the convenience of track selection without the damage to adjoining grooves. And, as a bonus to record collectors, in addition to the new CDs that are being released as repackages of recent just out-of-print LPs, there is now a renewed interest in releasing long out-of-print or previously unreleased material, including early rhythm and blues, rock and roll, rockabilly, jazz and country music. This means that the library that wishes to include recordings from as far back as the early 1920s and 1930s can build a workable collection without having to rely on out-of-print LPs, 45s, and 78s, and more are being released every week. As a bonus but as an expected and accepted component to these new CDs are the liner notes, which usually include discographical information, lyrics, historical and biographical essays. The only drawback to these booklets is their miniature size. Printing and pictures are often quite small and painfully tax the eyes of many users.

If a library so chooses to include recordings on the older formats, especially LPs, 45s and 78s it has a distinct advantage in acquiring material that in many instances will *never* be available on reissue. Small labels with ownerships lost to oblivion, major label issues of non-hit material, and the just plain weird. Weird includes material, usually on 45s, with songs about historic and some not-so-historic events and people. How many CD reissues will include songs about George Brett's pine tar on the bat incident, Patty Hearst's escapades, the death of soul singer Otis Redding, or LBJ's Beagle ear-pulling? And it goes without saying that record packaging on these earlier formats is most valuable to not only the student of music but also to students and researchers in art, sociology, applied human ecology (home economics and fashion), and psychology. LP covers offer especially wonderful graphic examples of social attitudes, artistic and photographic styles, and fashion statements and trends. LP inner paper liners and 45 rpm sleeves usually illustrate marketing techniques practiced by the record companies, including lists and advertisements of available recordings.

Selecting and buying recordings is an art that has to be developed through years of experience. When this author assumed his position at Bowling Green in 1967 he had already been personally collecting recordings for approximately 18 years, so that stepping into this new professional situation was eased by the fact that the intricacies of acquisition had already been honed. Sad to say the world of record buying from those mid-1960s, let alone the 1970s, and further back—the 1950s—is much different that it is today. Now most every new record store, some independently owned but many part of larger chains, carry CDs exclusively, with a side stock stock of both audio and music video tapes. No more 45s except a limited stock of newly pressed oldies, and a small browser bin or two with recently cut-out LPs that are pretty stagnant.

Thrift stores such as those operated by the Salvation Army, Goodwill Industries, the Volunteers of America, and St. Vincent DePaul, flea markets, and garage sales in the past have been wonderful sources for cheap recordings of all sizes and speeds (10¢ for 45s and 78s and 25 to 50¢ for LPs). These sources still exist but the selection has diminished, the prices are up, and 45s and 78s are almost a vanishing breed. They can still be shopped today but the treasures and sheer bulk of recordings is no longer there. Not that many records don't make it to these outlets. Years of passing do take its toll on the older items appearing as frequently, but that which is there is being bought up in greater quantities by an increasing number of informed collectors and dealers.

The dealers of which I speak are a new breed that cropped up in great numbers during the mid- to late-1960s and thrive by marketing all types of second hand recordings through mail-order, both set price and auction, used record shops, usually found in metropolitan areas and around college campuses, and record shows of collector conventions. The sale, barter, and trading of used recordings has actually thrived since the days of the early cylinder, especially strong though during the 1930s and 1940s with collecting of classic jazz and blues 78s and during the 1950s with a strong interest in rhythm and blues doo-wop vocal 45s. But now, with a newly informed collecting clientele, the record shop, mail auction, and record show prove to be the best sources for acquiring older LPs, 45s, and 78s.

A number of collectors' magazines which are still in print today offer a wide range of recordings for sale or by auction. One of the most widely read is *Goldmine* (700 East State Street, Iola, Wisconsin 54990). It carrys articles about musicians and collectibles, music news, reviews, editorials, and discographies (i.e. record lists by artist, label, or genre). And auctions with a set closing date, set sale lists, and display advertisements offer a wide range of recordings for a library to choose from if they are seeking out-of-print material.

Used record shops are havens for choice, bargain, and sometimes highly priced recordings. Most sell LPs exclusively but others carry 45s and 78s. There are others that *only* carry 45s or 78s. These stores are usually found listed in the aforementioned *Goldmine* and also the telephone yellow pages under Compact Disc and Phonograph Recordings—Retail. The records displayed in these stores usually are arranged by artist under broad musical styles and also by other general types such as shows, childrens, comedy and spoken word. Most stores also feature a "bargain" section where discs in less than new condition and "slow movers" sell from to 25¢ to $2.00. The regular stock usually sells from about $2.00 up, reflecting the dealer's knowledge of the used record trade.

Record shows, another gold mine of used recordings, feature the same stock as do the shops except for a smaller stock. The dealers that set up here are sometimes dealers with storefronts, other times they are private individuals that either sell out of their home or mail order. or they are people that are just trying to get rid of an accumulation of records. Both the stores and shows accept trades and/or cash for records. Shows, with dealers numbering up to a hundred at times, usually appear on a regular basis in established locations such as halls, closed storefronts, and church gyms. Admission is usually a dollar or two.

Not mentioned above but just as productive and quite cost-conscious is the acquisition of new and cut-out product from wholesale dealers. Most of these dealers are the middlemen selling to retail establishments and can furnish catalogs upon request. Their catalogs usually are quite large but are often arranged in such a manner that they can be perused with ease. Some list new product and catalog items separately with specials—including discontinued items—frequently included. Some catalogs are arranged by artist and title while others (to this author's joy) list them by label and number. One drawback to some of these companies however is that their orders must be prepaid. This means that unless an institution is willing to pay *proforma* business cannot be conducted with them.

The joy previously alluded to regarding label/release number order of dealer catalogs is so expressed because this is the only way to keep track of all the records in the library. A list with more information would be too cumbersome and when searching records either in a retail establishment or from dealer lists a quick but accurate method has to be adopted, and this is it. This same list can be taken to flea markets, record shows, and record shops alike with the same results. But a word of warning—keep it up to date and make it legible. There is nothing more depressing than to return to the library to find that the library already has the record. And another word of warning—when shopping for used records always check for condition and make sure the right record is in the container.

A final remark must be made concerning the acquisition of recordings through gifts. Donations, though not pre-selected, can and do become wonderful additions to the collection, and of course can save many dollars in the process. Arrangements with local radio stations can be made to pick up unplayed and played-to-the-end-of-their-popularity discs on a regular basis, usually monthly for the best selection. Collection drives can be initiated through the local city and student newspapers usually with a well-written article appearing once a year or so. A classified ad can also be placed but news coverage, if you can get it, yields the best results. And if the university has an alumni newspaper an article can also be placed there, describing the virtues of the record collection, with a plea for donations. The same radio stations mentioned earlier can also run public service announcements stating that the collection is seeking donations.

And finally, it should be easily surmised that not only with collection development activities but also with the other duties that are associated with creating and maintaining a recordings collection, the necessity of getting a 24-hour day into eight hours is perhaps the most challenging.

Picture/Shaped Discs

by Lisa L. Barker

What can you say about vinyl? Cast aside the obvious slams about sound quality and longevity, but with the exception of a little creativity on a label, vinyl is ... well ... ugly.

Around 1978, during the height of disco, record companies needed to spice up America's number one music format. Realizing some of the best and most original artwork was placed on a flimsy slab of cardboard, executives must have thought the cover would look better spinning around at 33 1/3 rotations per minute on a turntable. Hence was born the picture disc.

Actually picture discs had been around a few years before they caught on in the late 1970s. The earliest known "pic discs" were made in the late 1920s from RCA Victor. The oversized 78s featured art deco vinyl or caricatures of singers featured on the disc. "One of the most collectible from the era is a piece from jazz artist Paul Whiteman," said Bolingbrook, Illinois collector Gary Bernstein. The "live" recording is considered one of the rarest picture discs ever made and is valued at close to $1200.

In the 1930s, Mercury Records got into the picture disc business by releasing several classical and opera pieces, featuring opera scenes for vinyl art. "They also made some children's records," Bernstein said. "Those were done up with vinyl cartoons for the kids." The albums were shaped in various sizes and are valued at between $150-250.

Probably the best-known early picture discs came from Vogue recordings, between 1946-1947. The Detroit plant where the discs were manufactured burned to the ground in 1947, but in that length of time the company issued close to 90 picture discs featuring various vocalists and instrumentalists. "They featured artists such as Judy Garland and Glen Miller," Bernstein said. Avid collectors of the Vogue pieces said individual discs can sell for anywhere from $75 to $500. But the rarest picture disc of them all might only be linked to a story.

"Rumor had it is that someone at Vogue made a picture disc of Frank Sinatra," Bernstein said, "but supposedly only one was ever made and I think it was given to Sinatra." Collectors say the piece, if it exists, would be considered priceless.

Even though some picture discs from the last 20 years can be found in cut-out bins at used record stores, most have managed to keep their worth. "It's funny," said Charlie Essmeier of Retro Records, "The ones no one really bought then are the big sellers now." Essmeier uses the KISS solo picture discs (Casablanca 7120-7123) as examples.

"I guess they were going for about 50¢ in cut-out bins right after they came out and now I sell them for $50," he said

The picture disc regained its popularity in the mid '70s. But in the beginning of the decade, the resurgence of the format did not include Top 40 artists. Groucho Marx released a disc, *An Evening With Groucho* (A&M 3515) in 1972. Blues singer Mississippi Fred McDowell came out with a disc jockey promo picture disc, *I Do Not Play No Rock & Roll* (Capitol 403) the next year.

The rock 'n' roll genre began to take notice of picture discs after Paul McCartney & Wings released *Band On The Run* (Capitol 11901) in 1975 with a picture disc option. To most record buyers, it was the first picture disc they had ever seen, and before too long, a good portion of major artists got on the picture disc band wagon.

Dealers and retailers still manage to get a good price for artistic vinyl. Bruce Springsteen's *Darkness On The Edge Of Town* (Columbia 35318) has been selling in *Goldmine* for upwards of $100. "You would be surprised what still sells well," Essmeier said. "Cher's *Take Me Home* (Casablanca 7133-1979) gets about $40 still." Essmeier also admits that some of the most obscure pictured vinyl commands interest, including former "Wonder Woman" Lynda Carter, who's *Portrait* (Epic 35308) release can still be found on collectors' want lists.

Probably one of the rarest modern-era picture discs came from a disco-roller skating influenced fantasy-movie called *Xanadu.* Collectors say MCA Records allegedly made only 50 copies of the promo-only 10" single of the title song (MCA 2315). Other dealers say the record company destroyed about 12 of those copies, claiming they were defective. Whatever story you hear, all dealers say the disc, in mint condition, goes for about $600.

Another rarity, according to dealers, is the Supertramp *Breakfast In America* release (A&M 3730). The story goes that A&M presented select employees with a 12" copy of the album, complete with their pictures posed with the "waitress" on the cover. Collectors say the vinyl is very rare, since only about 25 to 50 actually exist. Dealers say the disc is worth, in mint condition in excess of $500.

Another rarity is courtesy of the Police. When the trio released *Ghost In The Machine,* there was allegedly a prototype, promo-only idea that was just that ... an idea. But according to collectors, the disc, which apparently lights up when rotated on a turntable, does exist, with only about three actually known of. Collectors say the album, if available, would go for about $1,000.

But not all picture discs from the era end up being more popular than when first released. Probably two of the most popular picture discs of their day, Bob Welch's *French Kiss* (Capitol 11663) and Meatloaf's *Bat Out Of Hell* (Epic 34974) go anywhere from $4-10.

Collectors say the best "obscure" buy is not the picture disc, but instead, its distant cousin the shaped disc. "Demand is very great," said dealer Jack Wolack. "They tend to disappear fast," Charlie Essmeier said. "They were not made in the mass quantity that picture discs were. People are intrigued by them because they are so unusual."

No one is sure which artist had the first ever shaped disc. Capitol issued shaped discs as far back as the mid 1940s. "I know there was a Bugs Bunny shaped disc that came out on Capitol during Christmas time," Bernstein said. "It was a flexy-cardboard disc with coating." He estimates the record, if found, could be worth close to $50.

Most people we talked to say the Police's *Roxanne* badge-shaped disc (valued at around $20-30) is one of the first "modern" shaped pieces, but unlike picture discs, current hit shaped discs are still being manufactured and can be found ... and are popular.

"One of the hottest shaped discs I've seen lately has been the Rush space shuttle," Essmeier said. The Canadian trio's release of "Countdown" off the *Signals* album is shaped like a rocket ship and is still very much in demand. "I usually sell out as soon as I get them," Wolak said. "Every Rush collector is looking for them," Essmeier said. "I have a waiting list," he added. According to retailers and dealers, the single is currently selling, when found, for anywhere between $125-150.

One of the many artists who enjoy shaped disc collectible popularity is Prince, who has come out with no fewer than a dozen different shapes to his credit. One of the more popular favorites among collectors of the Purple One is the motorcycle shape for the song "Purple Rain." Enthusiasts say only 1,000 were made and average in at about $120 a piece. "I'll be honest," Essmeier said, "The only stuff I can sell of his is the picture and shaped stuff."

Madonna shapes have also increased in price over the years. Dealers claim, whether you like Madonna or not, an investment in one of her shaped discs is a wise move. The Material Girl is another fan of shapes and has come out with just as many as Prince. Two of the more collectible pieces include the "Crazy For You," white bustier, selling for about $125 and the "Into the Groove," heart shape, selling for about $80.

When trying to track down your particular favorite artists on either picture or shaped discs, dealers have a word or two to the wise. "When you see it, buy it," said Wolak. "If you don't I will." Wolak says the best artwork usually makes the best investment. Picture that.

Picture Disc Listing

The following is a listing of rare and/or not readily available domestic picture discs. This is only a sampling and not a complete listing. (Thanks to Neal Umphred)

group	record #	title	year
Bee Gees	RSO 3042	Spirits Having Flown	1979
Boston	Epic 44188	Self Title	1978
	Epic 45050	Don't Look Back (DJ)	1982
Brothers Johnson	A&M 4714	Blam! (DJ)	1978
Glen Campbell	Capital 11722	Basic (DJ)	1978
Lynda Carter	Epic 35308	Portrait	1978
Cars	Elektra 576	Shake It Up (DJ)	1981
Cher	Casablanca 7133	Take Me Home	1979
The Clash	Epic 1595	Combat Rock (DJ)	1983
Joe Cocker	Asylum 145	Luxury You Can Afford (DJ)	1978
Elvis Costello	Columbia	My Aim Is True (DJ)	1979
Neil Diamond	Col. 39915	Primitive	1983
Earth Wind & Fire	Col. 035647	Best Of (DJ)	1979
Peter Frampton	A&M 3703	Comes Alive	1978
	A&M 4704	I'm In You (DJ)	1978
Judy Garland	Mark 56	Live In San Francisco	1978
Heart	Mushroom 5008	Magazine (DJ)	1978
	Columbia 884	Dreamboat Annie	1978
Levon Helm	ABC 4-5	Self Title (DJ)	1978
Pee Wee Herman	Fatima	The Pee Wee Herman Show	1981
Englebert Humperdinck	Epic 35020	Last Of The Romantics (DJ)	1978
Michael Jackson	Epic 38867	Thriller	1983
	Motown 6099	14 Greatest Hits	1984
	Epic 44043	Bad	1987
Jackson Five	Epic 34835	Goin' Places (DJ)	1978
	Epic 39576	Victory	1984

Jefferson Starship	Grunt 3363	Gold	1976
Waylon Jennings	RCA 3406	Greatest Hits	1979
Elton John	MCA 1995	A Single Man (DJ)	1979
	MCA 14591	A Single Man	1979
Judas Priest	Col. 39926	Great Vinyl & Concert Hits	1984
KISS (solo)			
Gene Simmons	Casablanca 7120	Self Title	1978
Ace Frehley	Casablanca 7121	Self Title	1978
Peter Criss	Casablanca 7122	Self Title	1978
Paul Stanley	Casablanca 7123	Self Title	1978
KISS	Mercury 832903	Crazy Nights	1987
	Mercury 836887	Smashes, Trashes & Hits	1988
Meatloaf	Epic 34974	Bat Out Of Hell	1979
Groucho Marx	A&M 3515	An Evening With Groucho	1972
Paul McCartney & Wings	Capitol 11901	Band On The Run	1975
Mississippi Fred McDowell	Capitol 403	I Do Not Play No Rock & Roll (DJ)	1973
Moby Grape	San Fran. 04830	Moby Grape '84	1984
Motley Crue	Elektra 60395	Helter Skelter	1984
Anne Murray	Cap. 11743	Let's Keep It That Way (DJ)	1978
Willie Nelson	Col. 35305	Stardust	1978
	Col. 38258	Always On My Mind (DJ)	1983
	Col. 39943	Always On My Mind	1983
	Col. 171010	Willie Nelson & Family (DJ)	1983
Olivia Newton-John	MCA 3067	Totally Hot	1981
Ted Nugent	Epic 99607	State Of Shock (DJ)	1979
Robert Palmer	Island 819	Secrets (DJ)	1979
Parliament	Casa. 7125	Motor Booty Affair	1979
Dolly Parton	RCA 1343	Great Balls Of Fire (DJ)	1979
	RCA 812	HBO Presents Dolly Parton (DJ)	1983
Teddy Pendergrass	Phil. 30595	Life Is A Song Worth Singing (DJ)	1978
Pink Floyd	Cap. 11902	Dark Side Of The Moon	1978
Elvis Presley	RCA 3078	A Legendary Performer (Vol. 3)	1979
Queensryche	EMI 1436	Operation Mind Control (DJ)	1988
Quiet Riot	Pasha 39203	Metal Health	1983
The Residents	Ralph 7906	Eskimo	1983
	Ralph 0001	The Mole Show	1983
	Ralph 0667	Meet The Residents	1985
Kenny Rogers	J. Rogers 5001	Backroads	1975
	U.A. LA934	The Gambler (DJ)	1978
	Liberty 8344	HBO Presents Kenny Rogers (DJ)	1983
Rolling Stones	R. Stones 39113	Still Life	1982
Linda Ronstadt	Asylum 401	Living In The U.S.A.	1978
Roxy Music	Atco 38114	Manifesto (DJ)	1979
Rufus	ABC 1049	Street Player (DJ)	1979
	ABC 1049	Numbers (DJ)	1979
Rush	Mercury 1300	Hemispheres	1979
Bob Seger	Cap. 11557	Night Moves (DJ)	1978
	Cap. 11557	Stranger In Town	1979
Bruce Springsteen	Columbia 35318	Darkness On The Edge Of Town (DJ)	1978
Starcastle	Epic 34935	Citadel (DJ)	1979
Barbra Streisand	Col. 1891	Yentl (DJ)	1983
	Col. 39909	Emotion	1985
Donna Summer	Casa. 7119	Best Of Live & More	1979
Toto	Col. 35317	Toto	1979
	Col. 36813	Turn Back (DJ)	1979
	Col. 37928	Toto IV (DJ)	1979
	Col. 39911	Isolation	1984
Stevie Ray Vaughan	Epic 39609	Couldn't Stand The Weather	1984
Bob Welch	Capitol 11663	French Kiss (DJ)	1979
The Who	MCA 14950	Who Are You	1979
Frank Zappa	B. Pumpkin 1115	Baby Snakes	1982

A Brief History of the Jukebox

by Fred Roth

The jukebox has been a phenomenon in the United States since its conception in 1906. Although it never really came into its own until the mid-1930s due to stiff competition from the nickelodeon and technical advances, it always did what it was supposed to do – rouse the curiosity of the passerby. After all, the main function of the automatic phonograph was to get the customer to part with some of his or her hard-earned money.

Early on, from about 1906 until the mid- to late twenties, most manufacturers learned that allowing a window for the patron to watch how the mechanism operated was as much of a money producer as the music itself.

Since amplification of sound had not yet been perfected, the few jukeboxes produced were acoustical in nature just like the early wind-up Victrolas. Sound was at best audible and the massive nickelodeons manufactured by Wurlitzer, Seeburg, and others were far superior to the jukebox which earned little share of the public's nickels.

That no one had yet discovered a material hard enough to manufacture a needle that could endure any more than two to three plays was also a problem during this period. The John Gabels Company of Chicago held patents on an automatic needle changer and because of this the company dominated the industry. By 1928 the amplifier was sophisticated enough to produce at least a sound as loud as a nickelodeon, and many companies began to enter the field.

1929 and the beginning of the depression saw an end to the nickelodeon because of cost, and the popularity of the jukebox increased. By the middle '30s competition was stiff. Such well-known companies as Wurlitzer, Seeburg, Rock-Ola and AMI joined ranks with pioneers like Mills, Gables, Capehart, Western Electric, and Electromuse for a share of the public's resources.

It was soon discovered that interest in watching the machine work was no longer enough to attract the borderline customer. Wurlitzer came up with the idea of adding colored lights in 1936. It worked, and by 1938 not one manufacturer had missed the boat. Each producer was trying to outdo the competition by making its phonograph a little more gaudy, therefore drawing the customers like a magnet to the product.

For the next 10 years the industry went through what is known as the Golden Age of Jukeboxes. Without a doubt the most beautiful phonographs ever built were produced during this period. Their design is so striking that many consider some of them works of art. Wurlitzer was fortunate to have working for it the greatest of all jukebox artists, Paul Fuller. During that 10 year period Fuller produced 13 different models for Wurlitzer, all of which are highly collectible machines today. Fuller's crowning glory was his design of the Model 1015 bub-

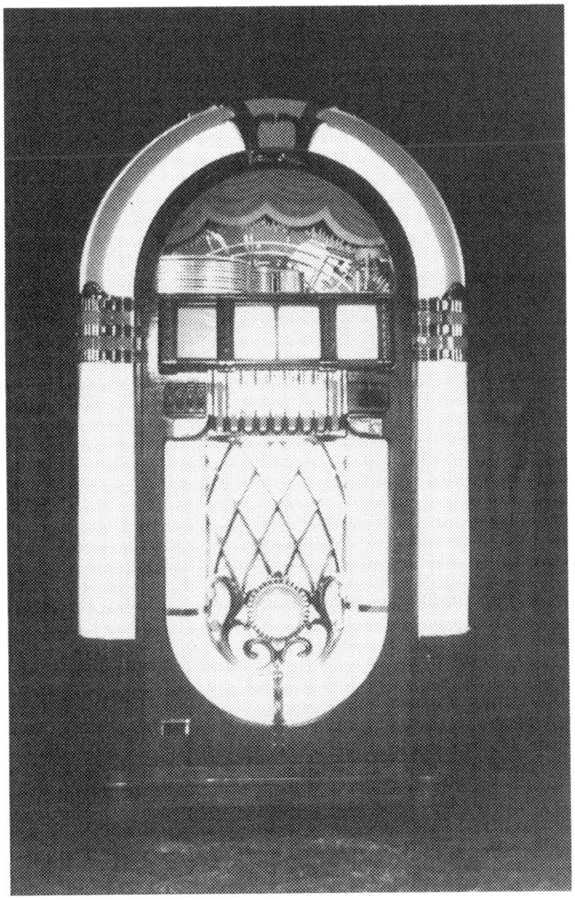

ble light machine produced in 1946-1947. When Americans thinks of a jukebox, most think of the 1015.

The color trend would have continued even longer had it not been that a new trend, variety of choice, emerged like a bomb in 1948 when Seeburg introduced a 100-selection phonograph. Since the Wurlitzer played only 24 selections in 1948, the company was caught off guard. It went from "industry leader" to almost bankruptcy in a year. Rock-Ola found itself in the same predicament and suffered a similar fate. Both survived along with AMI, however, and by 1954, competition between the companies was lively. Seeburg produced the greatest selection ever with its 200-play model starting in 1955. The variety of selections definitely took its toll on design, however, and the jukebox turned from beauty to simple function. Hence, the collectable value of such machines never materialized and have little interest even today.

The 1970s and '80s brought a decline to the shrinking industry. Wurlitzer, just before its demise in 1974, brought out a nostalgic model named the Model 1050. This was a last ditch effort to recapture its past glory. This phonograph was more expensive than the competition's and didn't sell well. It was a grand way to say good-bye from a company that had made coin-operated musical machines for close to 100 years.

The final chapter, according to some operators, is the giant-size television screen now prevelant in many venues which has drawn almost all attention away from the jukebox. Said one operator, "Woe to the poor fool that drops a quarter into a phonograph during a thrilling episode of *All My Children*."

Reprinted with permission from *Jukebox Collector*

For more information about jukeboxes and jukebox collecting contact:

Jukebox Collector, 2545 S.E. 60th Court, Des Moines, IA 50317. Phone: (515) 265-8324, FAX: (515) 987-5762. Magazine for jukebox collectors.

Victory Glass Company, 3260 Ute Avenue, Waukee, IA 50263. Phone: (515) 987-5765, FAX: (515) 987-5762. Free catalog.

The Smithsonian/Folkways Archives

by Richard Skelly

Tony Seeger fondly remembers the day he first discovered Folkways Records. He was in the sixth grade, living on 8th Street in New York's Greenwich Village, and working on a paper for school about India. He found a Folkways album of music from India in a record shop. Whole new vistas of folk music appreciation opened up to him on that day.

Today, Tony Seeger is curator of the Smithsonian/Folkways archives at the Smithsonian Institution's Office of Folklife Programs in Washington, D.C. Sitting in his office on the second floor of 955 L'Enfant Plaza, Seeger is polite and friendly, in contrast to the more serious nature of some scholars.

"My uncle is Pete Seeger, so growing up in the Village on 8th Street, I was familiar with folk music. But my interest in non-Western music began when I went out and bought a recording, by Folkways, of Indian folk music, and discovered on it the sound of the tabla and shenai when I was 12 or 13. Since then, I've had an interest in non-Western music as well," Seeger says.

Seeger adds that though he never met Moe Asch, the late founder of Folkways Records, Asch would often call for his uncle at his family's flat on 8th Street.

"He would always hang up the phone without saying goodbye," Seeger recalls with a smile.

"Folkways has always meant something to me, personally. It changed my life. And it was my uncle's record label," he says.

Seeger was happily running the Archives of Traditional Music at the University of Indiana at Bloomington and teaching anthropology and enthnomusicology there when he was tapped in 1988 for the job at Smithsonian. Seeger said then-secretary Ralph Rinzler called him and said, "'Wouldn't you really love to have this job?'

"So it was worth giving up the sabbatical I already had planned. Coming to Smithsonian as a scholar, I knew there were certain credentials I already had.

"And coming as a Seeger, I knew there were certain creden-

Woody Guthrie and Pete Seeger. Though there are many fine examples of their work readily available, the Archives at Smithsonian/Folkways contain vast quantities of unreleased recordings of these folk greats.

tials I had in the folk music world as well, outside of the institution. So I figured I was probably in a position to work it both ways, and I think I was probably right, being both a Seeger and involved in anthropology."

The collection of records, photos, tapes, acetates, correspondence and memorabilia that belonged to the late Asch, who founded Folkways Records in 1940, came to the Smithsonian Institution in 1987, after Asch passed away from a stroke in 1986. More than 3,000 recordings were made by Asch between 1940 and 1986, an average of one record a week for 46 years.

The archives of folk, jazz, blues and traditional and ethnic musics at the Smithsonian's Office of Folklife Programs was started about 25 years ago, when the first Smithsonian Festival of American Folklife was held on the Mall in Washington. Organizers arranged to tape performances at each music stage. Occasionally the taped performances were marred by jets flying overhead on their way to National Airport.

"We have tapes, taped interviews, slides and tens of thousands of photos from the annual Smithsonian Festival of American Folklife. So already here was an accumulation of traditional music performances by hundreds of performers from all over the world, and we added to that the Folkways collection of master tapes, artwork, correspondence and outtakes that Moe Asch had never released, as well as all the stuff he did release. We have enough unreleased Woody Guthrie material to release a whole new album of material of hits that has never before been released," Seeger says, noting that while his archivist Jeff Place knows a lot about the scope of the archives, it continues to surprise everyone in the office with new discoveries.

The heretofore unreleased Guthrie material is one such gem the archives has yielded, Seeger says, noting, "These were things that didn't fit on the albums in the old days."

Seeger says there is also much unreleased material by his uncle Pete, and that some of the material could find its way onto a Smithsonian/Folkways album as well.

"We have some old Sonny Terry and Brownie McGhee stuff, and in retrospect, Brownie was pretty happy with the stuff he recorded for Moe in the 1940s and 50s," he says, noting that he'll always discuss it first with the artist before releasing the material on Smithsonian/Folkways, the archives' record label, which uses Rounder Distribution to get its product out to the public. If the artist doesn't care for the material, Seeger says, he might argue that the material has historical significance.

As both curator of the archives and director of Smithsonian/Folkways Records, Seeger's job is two-fold: one, to preserve the music for the future, and two, to get it out to the people in a multitude of ways.

"I sort of ended up running a record label by accident. I'm much more trained as an archivist and scholar than I am as a label chief," he explains.

"Here at Smithsonian they had not been doing very much in the preservation of sound," Seeger says.

"Sound comes last in this museum, certainly before smell, but after vision and writing. And it's a more recent invention than painting and sculpture, so they hadn't been doing very much, other than the Smithsonian Press, which put out compilations through licensing agreements with record companies, such as *The Smithsonian Collection Of Big Band Jazz.*"

The Office of Folklife Programs maintains a warehouse in Rockville, Maryland, where the rest of the voluminous Folkways archives is stored, but just a look around the archives at the L'Enfant Plaza location reveals some 4,000 acetates of traditional blues, American Indian musics, French music, Yiddish songs, the music of Woody Guthrie, jazz pressings by Art Tatum, Stuff Smith, Joe Sullivan, Mary Lou Williams and James P. Johnson. Aside from issuing folk recordings, including a series of anthologies of jazz from New Orleans and other cities.

Walking through the archives, which also includes books and magazines about folk, jazz, blues and ethnic musics, archivist Place says the Smithsonian welcomes researchers and authors.

"Collectors and enthusiasts who have expertise in certain areas are welcomed, 'cause we still haven't been able to identify all of this stuff. A lot of things were put away in the wrong boxes," he says.

Seeger says that Asch would often record an artist's first one or two albums, as was the case with country/blues singer Lucinda Williams, or an artist's last few albums, as was the case with Big Bill Broonzy, who was dropped from a major company toward the end of his career. About one-third of the material that the Smithsonian/Folkways record company now issues is new material, mostly ethnic musics, while the other two-thirds is reissue material from Asch's vast archives.

"As far as the label goes, we're not really equipped to develop artists here at Smithsonian. That's being done very well by a lot of other labels. What's not being done is reissues or trying out new media and more educational materials. Current touring acts are being done very well by record companies like Flying Fish and Rounder. Of course, we'd love to have a rap group, if one volunteered," he says.

"We also do a series of recordings to coincide with whatever is happening at the annual Festival of American Folklife, and what I like about it here is we can collaborate with other academic institutions to put out new music that they think is worthy of being preserved. so right now, we're collaborating with the Indonesian Society of Performing Arts to put folk music from Indonesia that they want to have recorded and preserved," Seeger says.

Seeger notes that putting out quality reissue recordings is often harder than putting out brand new projects, such as the folk music of Indonesia. "You're often dealing with artists who recorded material at one time, and now you're talking about releasing it now, and there are all sorts of technological advances we've made since these recordings were made. So it presents a different set of problems than if you were recording it today, from scratch.

"For instance, with the New Lost City Ramblers, we had something where the recordings weren't very good, and the master tape was lost. So how do you track down a master tape? We got one from the French company on acetate, and that copy isn't quite as good, but you can recover some of it and in some cases, with reissues, you're just trying to determine who was singing on a recording. We were just listening to a tape that was marked Woody Guthrie, but in fact it was Pete Seeger. That wasn't what was on the box, and this poor researcher was here jotting down the words to the song, but with the wrong singer!"

Seeger says Smithsonian/Folkways works with several labs that specialize in audio restoration, which remove clicks and pops from noisy old acetates and wax cylinders so that people can enjoy the best fidelity possible.

A visit to the Smithsonian/Folkways Archives will reveal that the current collection is far more than a collection of Folkways recordings. Also available to researchers is a sizable collection of related books and magazines.

"We've also recently acquired and are about to put on line the collections of two other record companies, Cook Records and Paradon Records. Cook was a high-end audiophile label in the 1950s and 60s, and the man not only was a recording engineer, he also had his own pressing operation, to ensure high quality recordings. The other label, Paradon, was a topical music recording company from the 1970s, and it has mostly protest music, which adds to the depth of what we already have on Folkways," Seeger says.

The Smithsonian/Folkways Archives is open Monday through Friday from 9 a.m. to 5 p.m., and Seeger says, "We like to do things by appointment, only because we have a limited amount of listening equipment. One of the reasons we recently re-designed the whole archives was to give more space to the public. We answer inquiries by letter as soon as we can."

In terms of his job of both preserving the music and getting it out to the public, Seeger stays on top of the latest advances in computer technology.

"Eventually, I'd like to have it so that if there's any part of the Archives that you'd like, you can download it on your hard disc, from home, via your computer, after paying, so the artist gets a fee. I've always thought if we made this archives accessible to anybody, anywhere in the world, day or night, we'd *really* be doing a service to the general public."

To order a Smithsonian/Folkways catalog, or to contact Seeger or archivist Jeff Place, call or write:

Smithsonian/Folkways Recordings,
Office of Folklife Programs
955 L'Enfant Plaza, Suite 2600, Washington, D.C. 20560
FAX: (202) 287-3699, Phone: (202) 287-3262 for catalog:
Archives: (202) 287-3251.

The Rhythm and Blues Foundation

by Richard Skelly

Incorporated in 1988 and housed on the fourth floor of the Smithsonian Institution's National Museum of American History, the non-profit Rhythm & Blues Foundation has served as a guardian angel of sorts for otherwise forgotten blues and rhythm 'n' blues performers from the 1940s, '50s and '60s.

The rebirth in popularity of blues music in the mid-and late 1980s has prompted ever-growing numbers of rock 'n' roll artists and fans to become more aware of the roots of the music they love. Large blues festivals, books about the blues, ambitious blues and R&B reissue projects by dozens of record companies and the phenomenal sales of Columbia's Robert Johnson boxed set two summers ago are all strong indicators of a major blues renaissance.

So it seems fitting that in the last few years, the R&B Foundation should have grown in accordance with the public's renewed interest in roots music. Indeed, recent recording projects by Shanachie Records of Newton, New Jersey and Rhino Records of Santa Monica, California apportion a part of their sales royalties to the R&B Foundation.

Executive director Suzan Jenkins explains at her office that the R&B Foundation's purpose is two-fold: "We exist to provide financial assistance *and* public recognition for the legendary pioneers who were essential in the development of this rich American cultural heritage."

On a recent visit to her office, Jenkins explained how the organization formed: "There's an attorney here in Washington, D.C. named Howell Begle who represented Ruth Brown. It was about the time that Atlantic Records was having its 40th anniversary celebration. There was some discussion about her desire to receive her royalty payments, and it just came to the forefront," Jenkins says.

It was subsequently learned that there were many R&B artists who had not received their royalties, Jenkins says, not just from Atlantic Records, but from many different companies, so it was determined that a foundation should be established to address the needs of these artists, and an endowment of $1.5 million was procured through donations from Atlantic founder Ahmet Ertegun and the Atlantic Records Foundation. The R&B Foundation had a core group of founding trustees who made up the prime operational body, and Ertegun provided the group with the financial wherewithal to get started, Jenkins says.

"A lot of these artists were just beginning their careers when record companies were beginning their careers, too," she says, adding that most recording artists today don't have similar problems because the industry is older, presumably wiser, and all parties understand the more highly evolved royalty laws.

A string of successful fund-raising concerts was held in 1989 and 1990 to ensure the foundation's existence, but Jenkins stresses that the R&B Foundation "is not an arts presenting organization.

"Our mission is to provide financial assistance to artists from the 1940s, '50s and '60s, and it has never been part of our mission to continue presenting concerts. All of the funds we receive go directly to the artists. We're a service organization," she adds.

Through Begle's professional affiliations, the space at the National Museum of American History was found. Previously, the foundation had been housed at Begle's law offices in D.C. The museum received the collected works of Duke Ellington, and "it turned out the museum had long wanted to develop a deep and enduring relationship with organizations that highlight American music. Right now, they're in the midst of putting together an exhibit on the music of Memphis."

Aside from grant programs in excess of $2,000,000 per year to rhythm 'n' blues and blues artists in need, the R&B Foundation completes its mission in a number of ways. Its annual Pioneer Awards ceremonies during Grammy week recognize the artists whose lifelong contributions have been instrumental in the development of R&B music.

The foundation's financial assistance program, recently renamed "The Doc Pomus Financial Assistance Grant Program," in honor of the late songwriter, supports the current and specific financial needs of various R&B and blues artists. More recently, the foundation has begun working directly with the National Museum of American History's Division of Musical History, Division of Community Life, its Archives Center and Department of Public Programs to develop the History of Rhythm & Blues Collection.

But the foundation's most exciting project is one it has just started to work on, the creation of a Rhythm and Blues Archives. The foundation is working with the Smithsonian to establish a national Rhythm and Blues Archives that will be open to the public. When ready, the archives will eventually encompass a collection of R&B memorabilia, oral histories, film, videos and sound recordings. Plans call for the eventual production of a reissue series of mid-20th century recordings.

"It takes many, many years for a decent archives to be built, but since the Duke Ellington Archives is already housed at the National Museum of American History, it's that rich jazz legacy and the R&B legacy that we're bringing in here. It's a building process, but each time we receive some item of significance, it's hermetically sealed, so to speak, by experts at the museum, Jenkins says.

"We have already worked with the Smithsonian to produce a Resident Associate Program last year to highlight and present R&B as a historical integer in American music. It is our hope that we will continue to collaborate on many projects, the most ambitious one being the development of the R&B archives. We are hoping we can talk about the necessity of using an institution like Smithsonian to house the archives."

To receive the newsletter or to make a tax deductible contribution to help "preserve America's soul," write to:

The Rhythm and Blues Foundation, National Museum of American History, 14th and Constitution Ave., N.W. Room 4603, Washington, D.C. 20560

Goldmine Record Grading Guide

Records are graded by visual standards, not aural, the reason being that when purchasing a record at a show or through the mail the buyer does not get to listen to it. It should be borne in mind that visual evidence can be deceiving: the quality of the vinyl and the plating makes all the difference in the world. A record properly manufactured with a high quality plating may *look* VG+ and *play* near mint; this is particularly true of older albums from the '50s through the mid-'60s, when print runs were dramatically smaller, vinyl was fresher and more care was paid to the entire procedure. Albums from this period are a better investment in VG+ condition than the more recent American product. In fact, many albums from the '50s can be purchased in VG condition at reasonable prices and will play far better than the price paid would indicate. A record manufactured from recycled vinyl with poor plating (too many albums from the past 15 years or so) may look mint and play VG. Still, most high volume dealers do not have the time to listen to each item in their inventory, so visual standards remain.

When grading a disc, grade the overall wear of the vinyl. Always grade records under a good light. A 100-watt light bulb in a common desk-lamp will do a good job; most major defects will jump out at you and allow you to make an accurate assessment of the vinyl. Grading a record using light from the ceiling or from deflected sunlight entering the window will often "hide" paper scuffs, discoloration, groove wear and even some fingerprints. Always use a good, steady light source. Those of you who have attempted to closely examine vinyl records at a poorly lighted record show know how important good lighting is.

Finally, everyone makes mistakes in grading. It is easy to use a VG+ record as NM when you are attempting to sell it. This is a problem all dealers and collectors are prone to make and must be aware of. So don't condemn a dealer for one mistake; but, when the mistake is the norm, find someone else to buy your records from.

Mint (M)

Perfect. A mint record should appear to have just left the manufacturer without any handling; that is, it should appear perfect! No scuffs or scratches, blotches or stains, labels or writing, tears or splits; nothing. *Perfect.* And age has nothing to do with it; *the same standards for mint apply to a 78 from 1954 as to a major label's latest release!* There are no sliding values for mint. The single biggest complaint by collectors relating to grading over the years have been the deteriorating standards of sellers' grading. It is only natural for almost every one to turn immediately to the mint (read "highest") price in a price guide. If a record is mint-minus, take the assigned value and work you way down!

A mint album cover should appear to have never had a record in it; no ring-wear, dog-eared corners, writing, seam-splits, or even circular impressions, especially on single picture sleeves. a mint sleeve should essentially appear as though a record were never placed between its front and back covers! No slight seam splits, no turned down tops or dog-eared corners, no prices or dates stamped or written anywhere, including inside the sleeve. And, most importantly, no ring-wear! Any of these all-too-common signs of age would reduce the sleeve to VG+.

Ring-wear is defined as any imprint on the sleeve from the record that it formerly held. Any imprint. To many dealers and collectors the ink has to be worn off the picture for them to recognize the ring-wear and grade a sleeve down. Mint means perfect and nothing else.

Near Mint (NM)

A record that is otherwise mint but has one or two tiny, inconsequential flaws that do not affect the play or the appearance is "NM" and should command 90-95 percent of the mint price. For many, near mint and mint-minus mean the same thing; for the sake of this article, they remain interchangeable. When dealing with a seller who discriminates between the two grades, you should inquire as to what the dealer means when one record is referred to as "M-" and another "NM." Many dealers and collectors take the position that any used (opened) record cannot be verified as mint so they use NM (or M-) to describe what appears to be a perfect record that has been opened.

A sleeve for a single may have a slight impression from the record having been in it (no ring-wear; ring-wear should always be listed as a defect with the appropriate notation). An otherwise mint sleeve or cover with a price stamped on it is acceptable to many collectors; writing of any sort is not.

Similarly, LP and EP covers should still be close to perfect with minor sign of wear or age just becoming evident; slight ring-wear; minor denting to a corner; writing on the cover should all be noted properly.

Very Good Plus (VG+)

Sometimes referred to as "Excellent." A record that has been handled and played either infrequently or very carefully. That is, an item obviously not perfect, but not too far from it. On a disc, this could mean that there are slight paper scuffs from sliding in and out of a dust jacket; the vinyl may have lost some – not all – of its original lustre. A light scratch that did not affect the play in an otherwise nearly mint disc would be acceptably VG+ for most collectors; a scratch of any sort that audibly clicked throughout at a level greater than or equal to the music would not be acceptable. Always list the flaws in a VG+ record or cover. As a rule of thumb, a VG+ item is worth 50 percent, or one-half, of the near mint value.

On covers and sleeves, some wear from storage is acceptable, especially light wear that does not affect the beauty of the artwork. Again, listing the flaws when selling is safest.

Very Good (VG)

Used but not abused. A very good record will display visible signs of handling and playing, such as loss of vinyl lustre, surface scratches, groove wear, spindle trails from countless spins on the turntable. When played, surface noise will be evident, although it should not prevent the listener from enjoying the audio aspect of the disc. In other words, a VG record should appear to have been well-played although well-loved by a responsible owner. Gouges, rips in the label, cracks, maple syrups in the grooves are all unacceptable.

As more and more collectors spend more and more money, the lower limits of acceptability for an item to be admitted into their collection rises. That is to many collectors a record in "VG" condition is not acceptable unless it is truly rare and virtually unavailable in any other condition! And then, only if the price is scaled appropriately to match the condition. A "VG" record should command approximately 20-30 percent of the near mint price.

This is a difficult grade when discussing paper goods; usually a cover, like a disc, is VG when a variety of problems are evident. Ring-wear, seam splits, bent corners, loss of gloss on the photo, stains, etc. An aggravated combination of two of these problems—never all of them—would likely cause a sleeve to be graded VG.

Good (G)

Good in record collecting parlance all too often means a beat, trashed, take-it-to-the-flea-market frisbee. This should not be (obviously). Good should mean that the record is well-played with any number of defects that collectors normally shy away from, such as name labels stuck on the label, almost complete loss of surface sheen, aggravating surface noise, etc. Still, the purchaser, knowing full well that he or she is buying a "G" record, should be able to take it home, slap it onto the turntable and have a good time listening to it. Records that do not provide this most fundamental requirement are just no good. A "G" record should command 10-20 percent of the near mint price.

A good cover has seen considerable handling over a course of years and displays the obvious physical signs: ring-wear on the front and back, some seam splitting, particularly along the bottom and/or the left side, which would receive the brunt of the records sliding in and out; corners may be dog-eared to a light degree; an infatuated owner may have written his or her name somewhere; etc. Good should never mean bad. If a record or cover is beneath your contempt, it is not in "G" condition; look below for the appropriate guide.

Poor (P)

Any record or cover that does not qualify for the above "good" grading. A "P" record should command 0-5 percent of the mint price.

Record Collecting Abbreviations

Listed here are several common abbreviations used when advertising to describe flaws and their locations on a record or cover. Different collectors/dealers have different ways of using these abbreviations; some capitalize them ("DJ"), some use periods after each letter ("n.a.p.") and some use a slash ("c/o"). Those defects marked with an asterisk (*) should always be listed when advertising an item for sale or auction.

alt	alternate (take)
cc	cut corner*
co	cut out*
coh	cut-out-hole*
c-33	compact-33⅓ rpm single or EP
cvr	cover
dj	disc jockey, or promotional copy
ep	45 rpm extended play album
flexi	flexible plastic disc
imp	import
ips	inches per second
lbl	label
lp	12 inch 33⅓ rpm long playing album
mo	mono, or monaural
nap	(does) not affect play
ol	on label
org	original
pln cvr	plain paper jacket (no picture or titles)
promo	promotional copy
ps	picture sleeve
quad	quadraphonic
re	reissue
reel	reel-to-reel tape
repro	reproduction, or counterfeit
rpm	revolutions per minute
se	stereo effect electronically produced
2nd pr	second pressing
slt wrp	slight warp*
slv	sleeve
sm	saw mark (a cut-out mark)*
sm splt	seam split*
sol	sticker on the label*
sr	slight ring-wear on the front cover*
ss	still sealed
st	stereo
stkr	sticker
10"	10 inch 33⅓ rpm album
t&ts	(disc jockey) title & timing strip
toc	tape on the cover*
tol	tape on the label*
ts	taped seams*
wlp	white label promo
wol	writing on the label*
xol	an "x" is written on the label*